Attracting & Managing
VOLUNTEERS

A Parish Handbook

Donna Pinsoneault

Liguori

LIGUORI, MISSOURI

Published by Liguori Publications
Liguori, Missouri
www.liguori.org
www.catholicbooksonline.com

Library of Congress Cataloging-in-Publication Data

Pinsoneault, Donna.
      Attracting and managing volunteers : a parish handbook / Donna Pinsoneault. — 1st ed.
          p. cm.
      ISBN 0-7648-0717-X
      1. Lay ministry—Catholic Church—Handbooks, manuals, etc. 2. Parishes—Handbooks, manuals, etc. 3. Christian leadership—Catholic Church. I. Title.

BX1920 .P545 2001
254'.5—dc21   00-050648

Contents

CHAPTER 1

Send Down the Fire

TODAY IS THE DAY!

The feast of Pentecost is also Saints Alive Parish Volunteer Sign-up Sunday! This is the time of year when we ask all parishioners to volunteer to share their many gifts, their time and talent by signing up for one of our many parish ministries. Please prayerfully read the following verse then complete the form on the back by putting a check mark next to the ministries in which you are interested in serving. Thank you.

In a world ever shouting at us to do more! be more! get more!
Where do you want me to serve?
How will I know the right place?
the right time? the right gift to share?

Frankly, the thought of adding even one more thing
to my life…well…where on earth will I find the time…
the energy…the wisdom to be Kingdom NOW?

Just one little check on this piece of paper could change everything.
Am I…are we…ready for that?
At this moment, the best I can do, Lord, is this:
I am willing. We all are.

The rest is up to you.
Inspire us. Guide us. Fill us with courage.
Take us to that place where our deep gladness
and the world's deep hunger collide.
We ask this in your name, O Lord…
Send Down the Fire!

The place God calls you to is the place where your deep gladness and the world's deep hunger meet.

—FREDERICK BUECHNER

Below is a list of ministries that currently exist in Saints Alive parish. Check the ones for which you are interested in volunteering for a one-year term or more. Be sure to add your name and phone number. The committee chair will call you by September 1.

WORSHIP MINISTRIES
___ Liturgy preparation
___ Acolyte
___ Lector
___ Extraordinary minister
___ Bread baker
___ Usher
___ Choir
___ Cantor
___ Sacristan
___ Prayer group

SERVICE MINISTRIES
___ Neighborhood representative
___ Earth stewardship
___ Funeral receptions
___ Grief ministry
___ Food pantry helpers
___ Outreach committee
___ Interfaith network
___ Justice seekers
___ Meal program helpers
___ Senior citizen support

COMMUNITY-BUILDING
___ School volunteer
___ Athletic coach
___ Scout leader
___ Women's group
___ Men's group
___ Parish socials committee

FORMATION MINISTRIES
___ Catechist, preschool
___ Catechist, lower grades
___ Catechist, middle school
___ Catechist, high school
___ Youth ministry
___ R.C.I.A. sponsor
___ Small faith-sharing groups
___ Summer Bible camp program
___ Engaged couples' preparation team
___ Evangelization committee

ADMINISTRATIVE MINISTRIES
___ Building and grounds
___ Finance committee
___ Stewardship committee
___ Parish festival committee
___ Parish planning committee

Leadership Opportunities
___ Parish council
___ School committee
___ Athletic committee

OTHER
_____
_____
_____

NAME: _____ PHONE: _____

ADDRESS: _____

_____ Please check here if you are willing to be a committee chair.

During the homily, Glenna read the prayer printed on the front of the cherry red sign-up card twice, scanned the extensive list of available volunteer opportunities at the parish, then placed it on the seat beside her when everyone stood for the Creed. At the end of the pew Joshua Alexander, barely two, wriggled out of his father's grasp and scooted along the bench behind his family. He settled comfortably in the spot his mother had vacated, picked up the card, and put one corner of it into his mouth.

"No, Josh, mommy needs that," Glenna whispered.

She folded the card into her purse, pulled out a little plastic bag with a handful of Cheerios inside and gave it to Josh, then faced front again to recite with the others.

"We believe in the Holy Spirit, the Lord, the giver of life…"

"…We look for the resurrection of the dead and the life of the world to come. Amen." In the rear of the church, Bill pulled his card (completed, folded, and paper-clipped to his Sunday envelope) out of his breast pocket and headed to the front with the long-handled collection basket.

"What's wrong with these people?" he thought as parishioner after parishioner let the basket slide by without depositing either the card or their envelope. "Don't they get it? Don't they realize that the parish depends on their contribution of time, talent, and treasure?"

Bill knew the story. He'd chaired the finance committee for the last four years and before that served two terms on the parish council. He knew what it took to keep this parish running, knew the bottom line. He also knew that costs were rising along with expectations, while donations and volunteer commitments were falling off. That's why he'd insisted that, when the new deacon started on staff July 1, he would take on volunteer management as part of his job.

Back in his pew, Bill barely noticed the lady in front of him when he told her "peace be with you," but he noticed the Cheerio stuck to the chubby palm extended by the curly-haired tot with her.

Deacon Nate Morgan hovered at the side entrance to the worship space, waiting to make his appeal for volunteers. Formerly plant manager of a manufacturing firm that had been swallowed whole by an out-of-state conglomerate, he'd taken advantage of the generous early retirement package they had offered and applied to the seminary. Ordained a deacon in May, he'd hoped to be assigned to Crosstown, the faith community several miles east. With its healthy mix of African American, Hispanic, and Asian people, Crosstown had been his "home" parish for more than twenty years.

Instead, the bishop sent him to minister here at Saints Alive parish where nearly every face was white, and nearly every address was classy.

"Our hope," the bishop had written in his official letter of assignment, "is that you will bring your considerable experience and expertise to bear in supporting initiatives toward evangelization and collaboration."

At their first meeting several weeks ago, Father Ralph had echoed the bishop's sentiment. Then Father Ralph had told Nate about the extra little job they wanted him to take on. "We really need someone to beef up our volunteer program," he had explained. Then Father Ralph had asked Deacon Nate to make suggestions for the time/talent mailing and had invited him to speak at Mass on Pentecost to make a personal appeal.

Nate had taken Father Ralph's suggestions. He had reviewed the time/talent mailing and had moved the list of ministries to the back of the sign-up card and put a verse he liked on the front. He had had more ideas, but the look on parish secretary Marge Landowski's face told him he should keep the rest of his suggestions to himself.

Over at Crosstown parish, on the same Pentecost Sunday, Ramon was only listening with half an ear to the reading. He hated being here, hated that his mother had agreed to fill in for a co-worker during the Sunday morning shift at the hospital, hated that he had to bring Abuela now to Sunday Mass himself. At least he could be sure the guys wouldn't see him here propping up the old woman who dozed intermittently beside him.

Ramon hadn't set foot in the Crosstown parish church since his Confirmation ceremony two years ago and he'd only come then because his mother insisted. The crowd stood. Abuela leaned on Ramon's arm as she rose from her seat.

"On the evening of that first day of the week, even though the disciples had locked the doors of the place where they were for fear of the Jews, Jesus came and stood before them," the priest read.

Deacon Nate hadn't thought the rambunctious tot in the center section would make it through the homily without being scooped up by his frustrated mom and bodily transported into the vestibule. But there he sat, munching Cheerios contentedly as his family exited the pew and lined up for Communion.

Just before the closing hymn, Nate glanced at his watch, took a deep breath and headed for the ambo. He'd prepared his first speech to the parishioners carefully, pleased that it could be delivered in under five minutes. He'd also made sure that it didn't sound like one of those same old "share your gifts" appeals.

"Good morning, everyone," he began. Several small groups of people were filing out through the rear doors. The mother in the center section bounced her curly-haired boy on one hip and, with her free hand, held captive his youngest sister who was preparing to dart from the pew.

"I'm Deacon Nate Morgan," he continued, "and I'll take less than a minute of your time. As Father Ralph mentioned during his homily, Pentecost is an ideal time to think about all of the gifts with which you have been blessed by God and how you might share those gifts with your parish family. Last week you received a red time/talent sign-up card in the mail. If you haven't already done so, please fill it in now and leave it in one of the baskets at the entrances to the church. You'll find one or two extra cards in each pew. Thank you in advance for your help. I'm looking forward to getting to know all of you in the months to come."

Deacon Nate Morgan has just embarked on a journey for which he may be ill-prepared. Not that he hasn't studied a great deal about church. In the last three years, he's been totally immersed in courses on Scripture, Church doctrine, moral theology, and spirituality. Granted, he didn't give his full attention to the two-session course on parish management but, after more than two dozen years as a manager in a for-profit setting, he knew pretty much everything he needed to know about how to get people to get things done. Besides, he'd been a parish volunteer himself—many times.

How hard could it be to manage volunteers? He knew the three R's of volunteer management—recruit, retain, recognize. He knew that Saints Alive had a reputation for being a vibrant, dynamic parish. By rights, this part of his new job should be a piece of cake. In fact, he'd been surprised when Father Ralph described the parish's volunteer situation in such dismal terms.

The Truth About Parish Volunteering

Nate's situation is not unique. Though we talk a lot about vibrant parish communities, though post-Vatican II parishioners seem to understand that volunteer service evolves naturally from their baptismal call, though we've developed some pretty sophisticated sign-up techniques, in many parishes, volunteer ministry is just not humming along. Somehow, the reality of parish volunteers comes nowhere near to matching our vision.

Perhaps part of the problem is that we aren't clear about what that vision is. In fact, as Deacon Morgan heads home to his family after delivering his first recruitment appeal at Saints Alive parish, he might well be thinking about firming up that vision. During Mass, he had the opportunity to get a face-front look at the congregation. Something he saw, consciously or unconsciously, moved him to change his original ideas about the volunteer situation at Saints Alive parish.

Perhaps it was end-of-Mass restlessness. Perhaps it was a deepening awareness that parish-centered volunteering has to happen in the context of busy, varied lives. Or perhaps he sensed that managing parish volunteers was going to require something more from him than just finding warm bodies to fill slots. How much more was something he had yet to discover? A solid plan for how to approach the process could provide a real advantage.

How about you? Before jumping into the process of volunteer management, it makes sense to plan. Using the "Planner" tools integrated into each chapter of this resource can help you develop a workable strategy. You can work through them on your own, but working with a small group of other interested persons is more fun and usually boosts results.

Volunteer Ministry Planner 1: Envision "Thriving"

The best plans usually begin with discovering a long-range vision. The following exercises can help you get started on discovering a vision for volunteer ministry in your parish. You may wish to jot down your responses in a volunteer planning notebook that you have arranged for this purpose.

Envision people in your parish gathered for Mass. Describe what the group is like. Write down the first six words that pop into your head.

Now, try this exercise again. Imagine yourself observing people in your parish at Mass standing to recite the Creed. This time, focus in on people's faces. Try to see the expressions on their faces. Scan the faces of the rest of the congregation. Which of the words from the list below would you use to describe the group?

prayerful	energetic	happy	bonded
distracted	joyful	disinterested	involved
diverse	creative	reserved	respectful
connected	generous	comfortable	curious
restless	patient	friendly	kind
rested	sad	holy	engaged

Add any other words you think appropriate in your planning notebook.

> Hint: Imagine honestly. Look for and describe the bright spots, faces radiating enthusiasm. But don't ignore the not-so-bright spots, faces that seem distant, distracted, or downright disinterested. Describe the whole picture.

Now imagine the same congregation in a time when parish-centered volunteering is thriving. Now what do the folks look like when gathered to celebrate Eucharist? Write the words that would describe this group in your planning journal.

Pick words from your own lists or from the list below to write a brief vision statement for how people gathered for the eucharistic celebration will be different when parish-centered volunteer ministry is thriving.

"Thriving" Words

prayerful	friendly	involved	excited
energetic	listening	responsive	proactive
mobile	bonded	joyful	diverse
giving	creative	comfortable	peaceful
curious	patient	conversant	kind
rested	not in a hurry	known by name	happy
respectful	connected	eager	holy
generous	engaged	open to newcomers	loving

Now, in your volunteer planning notebook, write a simple vision statement that sums up how people gathered for Mass will act. Here is an example to give you some guidance. *We, the parish family of Sts. Joachim and Anne, a worshiping community, have as our foundation the teaching of Jesus Christ. We joyfully and responsibly call forth our gifts and eagerly and generously share them with all the members of our parish. We compassionately support the ministries which build up our community and the kingdom of God.*

> Hint: Consider this statement a rough draft. The best visions statements are clear enough to guide a planning process, but fluid enough to respond to the learning process.

A working vision statement is the first strategy step in effective parish-centered volunteer ministry. Use this vision to guide you as your plans evolve.

Practical Matters 1

Make Your Vision Visible

Having a vision toward which you can direct your efforts is important, but you won't get the most out of your vision until it becomes visible to others. Start making your vision visible whenever you communicate with current or prospective volunteers. Become aware of subtle and not-so-subtle messages in what you say, write, and print.

For example, turn back to page 2 where ministries currently available at Saints Alive parish are listed. Looking at just this list, minus the quote at the top and the verse that Nate added to the front, check off the messages that recipients would be likely to pick up from that mailing.

_____ They really want me to volunteer.
_____ They really need me to volunteer.
_____ They want to use me as a volunteer.
_____ I will get a response if I sign up.
_____ I might get a response if I sign up.
_____ They really appreciate their volunteers.
_____ Volunteering will benefit me.
_____ They really know me.
_____ This sheet came from a real person.
_____ This sheet came from a computer.
_____ They really want me to respond.
_____ They really know and respect me.
_____ They really value me.
_____ They really understand my life.
_____ They really see me as one of God's people.
_____ Other responses: _____

Deacon Morgan had added the quote at the top of the page, moved it to the back, and added a verse and graphic on the front. Do the additions change or add anything to the message? What is your opinion? Write your response in your volunteer planning book.

Quick Tip: Many people say that a simple story or verse makes even the most routine form seem more spirit-friendly, more conversational and intimate, and encourages people to be more open to possibilities.

Micro-Perspective

In the first part of Chapter 1, Nate visually met several parishioners who had received the sign-up form in the mail and had been expected to bring it with them to Mass on Sunday. Picture a member of the parish council receiving the letter and form in his or her mail. Check how likely the recipient will do any of the following.

Open It: ___ Very likely   ___ Somewhat likely   ___ Not likely

Complete It: ___ Very likely   ___ Somewhat likely   ___ Not likely

Return It: ___ Very likely   ___ Somewhat likely   ___ Not likely

Write your reasons for your response in your volunteer plan book.

Now picture Glenna receiving the same mailing in her stack of daily mail. How likely is she to do any of the following?

Open It: ___ Very likely   ___ Somewhat likely   ___ Not likely

Complete It: ___ Very likely   ___ Somewhat likely   ___ Not likely

Return It: ___ Very likely   ___ Somewhat likely   ___ Not likely

Write your reasons why in your planning book.

At Mass, Glenna realizes that she forgot to fill out and bring her sign-up form. How likely is she to complete and return the card today?

___ Absolutely   ___ Most likely   ___ Maybe   ___ Probably not

Write your reasons for your response in your planning book.

Now answer these questions. Jot your responses in your volunteer planning book.

- What print materials and forms do you use to invite people into parish-centered volunteering?
- How do they make your vision visible?
- Picture a person who is actively volunteering in the parish. Imagine that person receiving your parish's volunteer sign-up materials with their daily mail. How likely is the recipient to open the mailing? Complete it? Return it?
- Picture a person who isn't currently volunteering. How likely is he or she to open the parish mailing? Complete it? Return it?

Quick Tip: Don't be discouraged if sign-up responses from a parish-wide mailing or form distribution are small. "When I see something from the parish in my mail, unless it's my year-end contribution statement, I just toss it," said one parishioner.

That response is typical. When we use sign-up forms as our primary means of motivating busy, uninvolved people to volunteer, we are expecting nothing short of small miracles. When we think it through, the people who are most likely to respond to parish-wide mailings are people who are already invested in parish life. Those who are not already invested in parish life may not even open the envelope, much less take another step and complete the card. The responses we *do* get are wonderful gifts. Rejoice and give thanks for them all for they are already making visible that thriving parish you are envisioning!

CHAPTER 2

The Gift of Fire

Monday morning after Pentecost Sunday Nate returned to the parish office and found two baskets stacked behind Marge Landowski's desk. The number of sign-up cards inside seemed considerable, but Nate knew it came nowhere near to matching the number of people who had been at Mass on the weekend.

Nate pulled a handful of cards from the top basket and scanned them quickly.

"How long before they're all sorted?" he asked. "I want to get started on follow-up."

"Couple, three, weeks. It's not hard, but a volunteer comes in this afternoon to start keying responses into the computer," Marge said. "Pretty much the same people sign up for the same things every year. It's a matter of cross-checking the cards with what's already in the database, then making additions and deletions. Once the volunteers get the information into the computer, I print out lists of the committees people say they want to work on and give them to whomever oversees that committee. They do their own follow-up."

"What do we do about the people who haven't sent in a card?" Nate asked.

"Nothing."

"Nothing?"

"That's the way we've always done it." said Marge.

"I'd like to have two lists," Nate told her. "A list of all the folks who sent in a card along with their phone numbers and whatever else your database will print out. Then I want the names and phone number of all the parishioners who didn't send in a card."

Marge pulled a blue paper-bound booklet out of her desk drawer. "I'll give you copies of all the printouts the staff gets." She handed him the booklet and smiled sweetly. "When you have time, you can check them against the names in this parish directory. I'm only here mornings."

Before he left, Nate typed an announcement for the parish bulletin. "Thanks to all the parishioners who signed up last Sunday to help with one of the parish ministries, committees, or activities," it read. "Everyone who did not sign up is invited to a meeting Monday at 7:00 P.M. in the church hall. You will learn what volunteer opportunities are available here and why your help is so important to our parish. Questions? Call Deacon Nate Morgan at 411-555-6072."

"Better move your meeting back a week," said Marge when he handed her the copy. "Next Sunday's bulletin went to the printer first thing this morning."

Nate made a face and Marge repeated, "That's the way we always do things around here."

The Way It's Always Been Done

Why do we do things the way we do them in parishes? Many of our choices come from a firm commitment to live out our faith in accordance with Catholic tradition. But things like bulletin articles, deadlines, how databases are compiled and distributed, who gets what information when, also tend to be done the same way year after year. Before long, the way we do things comes to be viewed as the way parishes are supposed to do things.

Unfortunately how we recruit and manage volunteers may also fall into that category. Influenced by deadlines, software design, and organizational charts, the forms, invitations to service, and follow-up approaches have become accepted as official practices of parish life. Tacking phrases like "sharing your gifts" or "being good stewards of time and talent" onto recruitment forms miss the point even if they do make our forms sound a bit more spirit-friendly.

Why did the "check off the committees you are interested in" recruitment procedure become so accepted? One reason is that, in the United States, our view of how to best manage paid work shapes how we manage volunteer work. Even a brief look at the evolution of workplace management through the last century demonstrates how shifts in for-profit management theory have influenced how we manage volunteers.

On the Farm

Before the Civil War, work in a largely farm-based society was driven by the requirements of the season. Large landowners relied on slaves or low-paid seasonal workers, while small independent farmers counted on extended families to share the work load. Everyone, including children, were expected to do whatever was needed to get the seed planted or the crop harvested. When disaster struck, they worked harder and looked to God for help. "Volunteering" was everywhere, but not labeled as such. It happened informally, person to person, neighbor to neighbor, in response to observable needs. Barnraising and quilting bees are examples of how whole communities pitched in to help others.

Folks on farms and in towns saw their parish first as a place for worship, then as a site for social get-togethers. If their pastor or one of the parishioners heard that someone was ill or was laid up with a bad back, the word was passed and the family got meals or helped with the chores until they were back on their feet.

Father said Mass, taught religion, married young folks, baptized babies, and anointed the dying. When the church needed a new roof, male parishioners agreed on a work date, brought materials, and put it on, while the women brought sandwiches and other food. The message from the parish was, "Please help whenever help is needed. You know how."

Into the Factory

After the Civil War, work was driven by the requirements of profitable production. As the factory system emerged, workers were seen as inexpensive commodities who could be trained to perform repetitive tasks and who were expected to put in long hours for survival wages in order to increase profits for an owner they might never meet.

Meanwhile, ideas about the right way to manage were evolving. Work was driven by cumbersome rules, clear divisions of labor, detailed authority structures, impersonal work environments, and lifelong commitment to one's job and employer. Time/motion studies scientifically determined the "one best way" to do each task. Machine-like workers were expected to obey their superiors, sacrificing trust in their own resourcefulness to order, efficiency, and consistency. When questions arose, people looked to the owner for the answer.

Young people from the farm followed the promise of work into the city. No longer known by their neighbors, individuals and families in the burgeoning urban population struggled alone to make ends meet. Sensing great growing need, people with a deep desire to do good voluntarily opened shelters, meal centers, and orphanages to help the poor, the hungry, and especially, the children. Organization in these movements was informal but had unwritten rules.

Parish priests began to encourage parishioners to get involved in groups like the St. Vincent de Paul Society which was founded to take some of the burden of helping the poor off the shoulders of pastors who, as parishes grew, were beginning to struggle with work management issues of their own. Volunteering was viewed as a way to help the pastor get his work done. Educated women in religious orders taught the children full-time often in exchange for little more than room and board. Along with one or two men who advised the pastor on financial matters, an invisible handful of holy married women and widows comprised the entire volunteer work force in a parish.

During the depression, some parishioners volunteered to help in new organizations like the Catholic Worker Movement. Many, however, were struggling to keep their own heads above water. Though parish-organized volunteer opportunities were limited for most laypersons, society-organized opportunities were increasing. The message from the parish was, "You should help. Someone will tell you how."

Winners!

After World War II, work was driven by system-wide strategies designed to win market shares from competitors, a situation that required certain workers to be educated as managers. Though many more people earned high school diplomas before entering the workplace, a college degree became the instrument that really sorted those who gave orders from those who took orders. Certain tasks had to be repeated in every department, but work specializations emerged. Since "success" in any area now could be measured by "the numbers," the manager's job was to make sure that workers produced more faster.

In the parish, as Catholic schools overflowed with "boomer" babies taught by habit-garbed nuns, new parish volunteer opportunities surfaced. Walter, who had converted from a Protestant denomination when he married a parishioner's daughter, joined the men's society and, every Sunday, put two dollars from his wages in a preprinted envelope. When he went to church, he dropped it through a slot on a big wooden box near the entrance. The sign on the box read "Visitors' Offering—25 cents."

One November, he left his good suit on after Mass for three consecutive Sundays and went door to door seeking pledges for the new parish buildings. Every Saturday morning he drove his widowed neighbor to the market. After that, he took the Chevy to the local service station and talked with the green-uniformed man who filled the tank about what was happening in Korea. After the big new church and school were dedicated, his friend Bill, who sold insurance, asked him to become an usher. Walter declined saying that he didn't think that would be right for a convert.

Meanwhile, Walter's wife Helen joined the parish's women's society. She went to committee meetings and helped run bake sales for the school association. She also served as a scout leader, single-handedly guiding more than thirty eighth grade girls through the requirements of the Marian Award. Roles were clear. The pastor ran the church; the Sisters ran the school, with the pastor's permission, and trained a dozen boys or so from each grade to serve Mass. One of the Sisters played the organ and rehearsed the choir; a handful of men helped the pastor run the finances; some of the women helped with tasks that were considered too menial for people God had chosen to do important work. When questions arose, they turned to the pastor for the answer. The message from the parish was, "You should help the parish; we'll tell you how."

Turned Around and Upside Down

Long before re-engineering made headlines in the business world, Vatican II redefined how work would be accomplished in the Roman Catholic Church. No longer seen as simply receivers of the work of the Church, that vast group of believers known as the laity were to share in the Church's mission. Pope John XXIII called ordained Church leaders to come to the window and see the laity as having a real role in carrying out the mission of the Church.

Over the next decade, altars were turned. Well-worn Latin/English missals that had rested on pew seats while their owners knelt at a long, padded rails to receive holy Communion were replaced by paper-covered missalettes that people carried forward during the Communion procession so they could sing all the verses of the new songs they hadn't heard often enough to commit to memory. Laypersons began to take on some of the pastor's responsibilities. Though they had never set foot in a seminary, some parish members found themselves coming forward from the pews to read Scripture aloud during Mass, planning eucharistic celebrations, using words like "liturgy," "catechesis," and "baptismal call," and discussing social justice issues at parish meetings. Men were elected or appointed to the parish council which was responsible for fund-raising efforts, parish planning, and certain areas of decision-making. Nearly every parish organized outreach ministries, often resulting in overlapping services to popular community agencies while ignoring the less well-known. When questions arose, they created a dialogue to discuss the issues. The message from the parish was "Everyone wants to help; the community will show you how."

By the 1980s, Americans were catapulted into the "information age." Technology provided instant access to data and quantitative measurements, changing the way we worked in factories, on farms, and in offices. Companies began to need large numbers of workers with new kinds of skills. Recognizing that many U.S. producers were losing their competitive edge worldwide, management emphasized globalization and quality over efficiency, turning even century-old organizations upside down. Many Americans were "downsized" out of their jobs, as companies struggled to become more profitable and efficient. By the end of the twentieth century, people expected change to be inevitable in their organizations and in their lives.

The Gift of Fire

With change consuming all our ideas about the best way to do something, organizations had no choice but to operate with a "process" approach to management. Workers made decisions, provided input on how things should be done, cooperated in teams, collaborated with other teams, and took on a project orientation. Having experienced worship in new ways since Vatican II, having become more familiar with the Old and New Testaments, having lived through relentless change in their personal and work life, Catholic parishioners slowly achieved a certain level of comfort with another word that they hadn't heard used in Catholic circles for generations: "evangelization."

What happened at the first Pentecost happened again. Ordinary people came out of hiding behind the "should" and "supposed to" pillars that supported their image of personal holiness to tell their own story of encountering Jesus in the day-to-day world. But, for some of those people, the way we "always" did things in parish life—especially the way we managed parish-centered volunteering—no longer made sense.

The following Monday, Nate plugged in the coffee pot at 6:30 P.M., put out more sign-up cards and waited. By 7:00 P.M., no one had arrived. So Nate walked out into the vestibule to see if anyone was looking for the meeting room. A gray-haired woman was standing near the table where the leftover parish bulletins were kept.

"Are you looking for the meeting about parish volunteering?" Nate asked.

"Oh! No!" the woman said. "I'm just here to pick up a bulletin."

"I'm Nate Morgan, the new deacon here." He extended his right hand.

The woman's face reddened as she responded, "Adele Zachary. I…uh…didn't make it to Mass Sunday."

"Well, since you're here, Adele, how about having a cup of coffee with me? It seems I planned a meeting on a bad night and I've got a full pot brewing."

Adele bit her lip and said, "I guess I could stay for a few minutes."

As they headed toward the church hall, Nate asked Adele what she liked best about the parish.

Adele's Story

"I haven't been around here much," she said. "My husband was taken ill about a year after we moved here. He died last September."

"I'm sorry to hear that." Nate filled a cup with coffee and handed it to Adele.

"I don't know much about the parish except what time Masses are," Adele went on. "I probably should have gotten more involved, but I was really busy working and taking care of my husband."

Nate brought his own cup to the table where Adele was sitting. "That's understandable. I hope the parish helped you out some."

"We wouldn't have asked the parish to help," Adele said. "People here hardly knew us! When George was in the hospital last summer, someone brought Communion most Sundays. Other than that, you are the first person in the parish who's talked to me."

"You're kidding!" Nate said. "How long have you been a member?"

"Sixteen years."

Nate could hardly hide his surprise. He talked with Adele for nearly an hour about her husband's illness, her grown son in another state, her part-time job at City Hall. He told her a little about his own wife and daughters, about how much he was looking forward to his first assignment as a deacon.

Adele carried her empty cup to the trash can. "I'm not surprised no one showed up for your meeting," she said. "You have to invite people personally if you really want them to come to something. Even then, they won't come if they think they will be roped into working."

"I don't suppose you'd like to volunteer for a ministry," Nate said, unplugging the half-full pot.

"I haven't the foggiest idea what I'd do," she said. "I don't know a thing about ministry."

Nate smiled at the irony of her statement. "Why not help me? Help me get things organized."

"I could give you a couple of hours on Monday nights," Adele said.

"Perfect," Nate agreed. "I'll take whatever time you can give. I need you."

Nate walked Adele to the door. Before he left for the evening, he wrote thirteen notes by hand, twelve to the first dozen names under "A" in the parish directory, and one to his good friend Rosa Martinez. A cracker-jack volunteer at Crosstown Parish, he knew Rosa would have a lot to contribute to the discussion. Here is an example of the note Deacon Nate wrote:

Dear Joe and Kathy Abuchio,

I am the new deacon at Saints Alive parish and part of my job is to coordinate parish volunteers. Please be part of a conversation I'm planning. We'll meet in the parish hall on Monday, July 17 from 7:00 to 9:00 P.M. I am not trying to get you to sign up for anything. I just want to get your ideas and opinions about volunteer ministry in the parish. Please call me if you can't come. Otherwise, I will look forward to seeing you at 7:00.

Sincerely,

Deacon Nate Morgan

Volunteer Ministry Planner 2: Claim Your Purpose

After the participants at Deacon Morgan's conversation on parish-centered volunteering hash through their good and not-so-good experiences as volunteers, someone is bound to raise the question: "Why? what's the purpose of parish-centered volunteering?" How would you answer that question? Record your thoughts in your plan book.

On page 7, you drafted a vision statement to guide your planning for parish-centered volunteer ministry. A well-thought out vision acts like a beacon. It can't control your journey, but by keeping it in sight, you know you are headed in the direction you intended to go.

Keeping your mission in mind helps you focus on why you want to go there. Twenty-first century parishes are complex organizations. Today's typical parish not only supports the sacramental life of God's people in its neighborhood, it runs or cooperates with other parishes to run state certified schools, maintains extensive facilities, teaches religion to children who attend public schools, coordinates a wide range of outreach efforts, organizes activities and support for persons over their life span, hires employees, raises and disburses more money than some for-profit corporations do, and more. With so much going on, it is easy to lose sight of our primary mission as the Church: evangelization.

Evangelization is not just about spreading the Good News, Reverend John E. Linnan, C.X.V., Ph.D., told a group of Midwestern business leaders in 1998. "It is about making the world Good News for the people who live in it."

Linnan, professor of theology, former president of Chicago's Catholic Theological Union, and former board member of Milwaukee's Saint Francis Seminary said that the way the Church currently organizes its pastoral care is not working because most of the work falls to six to ten percent of the Catholics in an area while nearly fifty percent make little contribution past their weekly envelopes.

Though more people seem to be seeking a deeper spiritual dimension in their lives, Linnan said that many people say they do not find that dimension in the Church. Linnan encourages today's parishes to recognize that the Holy Spirit speaks through all people who seek God. He believes that, while clergy need to ensure the authenticity of faith, worship, and life of the community, they do not need to have an exaggerated sense of responsibility. Instead, they can return the church to the people, holding them accountable for operating it in ways that focus on the absolute centrality of Jesus, renewing their sense of mission, and making sure that Jesus is the organizing spiritual principle. To be effective, that effort may need to be supported by new structures, new modes of communication, and new styles of leadership.

"The whole point is to empower each of us for the evangelizing mission of the Church," Linnan said. "If that's not happening, something is very wrong with what we are doing."

How might someone who shares Father Linnan's point of view describe the purpose of parish-centered volunteering? Write your thoughts in your volunteer planning book.

As a person who manages volunteers, your first job is to help people come to a shared understanding of how parish-centered volunteering can help the parish be the parish it hopes to be. That happens when you make the vision of a how the parish is different when volunteer ministry thrives visible to others.

The next step is to help people come to a shared sense of mission around parish-centered volunteering. Whether debates over the role of the laity in Church leadership roles continue (or not), one message from Vatican II remains clear: all of God's people share in the Church's mission to evangelize. That being the case, the purpose of parish-centered volunteering is considerably broader and more significant than simply getting done what a pastor and/or the staff don't have time for or aren't being paid to do.

In your own words, how does volunteer ministry help the Church live out its mission? Give some thought to crafting a good response.

After Vatican II, many parishes adopted planning approaches that included drafting a mission statement. Parish councils took the lead in drawing a common understanding of mission from people in the parish, then put that understanding into words. These statements can be long or short. Some of those statements just hang on the wall. In other parishes, they are used as a tool to measure the effectiveness of parish decision-making.

As a person who manages parish volunteers, you are accountable for keeping the parish's mission in mind, doing all you can to further it and guarding against taking any action that might move the parish farther away from its fulfillment. While you don't have to commit long mission statements to memory, it makes sense to know its essential elements by heart.

- What are the essential elements of your parish mission statement? Write this statement in your plan book.
- Keeping your vision, the mission of the Church, and your parish's mission statement in mind, draft a statement that clarifies the purpose for thriving parish-centered volunteer ministry. As when you wrote a vision statement, expect this purpose statement to be firm enough to guide your planning process, but flexible enough to respond to what you learn.
- Now consider the primary purpose of striving for parish-centered volunteer ministry. Write that purpose in your notebook.
- Now rephrase that statement in terms of your own goals. As someone who manages volunteers, what is my mission?

> Hint: Strategic planning facilitators encourage people to draft mission statements that are no longer than ten to twelve words.

Practical Matters 2

Keeping Your Mission in Mind

Take another look at the volunteer sign-up form used by Saints Alive parish on page 2. How clearly does the Saints Alive sign-up form convey a sense of purpose for parish-centered volunteering overall? Very clearly? Somewhat clearly? Not clearly at all?

- The sign-up form has several parts. Circle the part listed below that most clearly conveys the purpose for parish-centered volunteering?

Form title   Directions   Verse
Quote   Ministry list   Personal information
Other: _____

- What main dominant purpose does the sign-up form convey? Write your thoughts in your notebook.
- Now find a copy of *your* parish's most recent volunteer recruitment form. How clearly does it convey the purpose for parish-centered volunteering overall? Very clearly? Somewhat clearly? Not clearly at all?
- What parts can you find in your current form? What purpose does each convey?
- How well does the form you are currently using align with the purpose statement you wrote on page 20 earlier in this chapter? Is it a perfect match? Close, but not quite there? Good start? Total mismatch?

Quick Tip: Avoid mixed messages whenever you communicate about parish-centered volunteer ministry. If all you are looking for are people to complete specific tasks, then ask for that without confusing your request with the experience of "baptismal call" or "sharing gifts from the Spirit."

On the other hand, when you see a volunteering experience as a way of discipling and the volunteering laity as a critical component of the twenty-first century Church, then be sure that message comes through loud and clear.

While we are reviewing the status quo, consider the following chart that summarizes how approaches to work management evolved through the last century. As in most contemporary organizations, parish work is usually managed by drawing elements from each approach. Circle any element that currently influences how volunteers are managed in your parish. Now is not a time to determine whether one approach is better than another, only to identify how you tend to do things around your own parish.

TWENTIETH CENTURY APPROACHES TO VOLUNTEER MANAGEMENT

	FARM-BASED	TRADITIONAL	FACTORY-BASED	PROCESS
NEEDS	Met directly	Met directly	Met indirectly	Met in terms of Volunteer needs
HOW?	1 to 1/group to group	1 to group	agency to 1/ agency to group	flexibly
COMMITMENT	Interpersonally defined	Organizer defined	Defined by organization	Project defined
JOB	Informally defined	Organizer defined	Defined by organization	Project defined
MANAGER STYLE	Neighbor	Organizer/controller	Task completer	Relationship builder
MESSAGE	"Please help… you know how."	"You should help… someone knows how."	"It's your duty to help. We'll tell you how."	"You want to help? Tell us how."
EXAMPLE	Barnraising	Catholic Worker Movement	St. Vincent de Paul Society	Human Concerns Committee

On the continuum below, put an X on the spot that most accurately describes how parish leaders tend to approach volunteer management overall.

Farm-based   Traditional   Factory-based   Process

Micro-Perspective

- Picture a person whom you know who is already volunteering. What management style most accurately describes how you are likely to manage that person's volunteer work: Farm-based? Traditional? Factory-based? Process?
- Now picture a person whom you know who is *not* currently volunteering. What management style most accurately describes how you are likely to manage that person as a volunteer: Farm-based? Traditional? Factory-based? Process?

> Quick Tip: People in the same parish who coordinate the work of volunteers may prefer one management approach over another. The same person may tend to manage one volunteer's work differently than that of another.

- It is very important to recognize your personal approach to managing volunteers. Your style may differ from that of other volunteer managers or from the overall approach in your parish. What approach most accurately describes your overall approach to volunteer management: Farm-based? Traditional? Factory-based? Process? Combination?
- Keeping your vision and purpose in mind, in your plan book, list any elements from the chart that you would like to incorporate into most of your volunteer management efforts.
- Keeping your vision and purpose in mind, list any elements that you would like move toward *eliminating* from most of your volunteer management experiences.

Keeping both sets of elements in mind will help you create a more effective plan for parish-centered volunteer ministry that's driven first by purpose, then by task.

CHAPTER 3

People With Coats

This time people showed up for Deacon Morgan's meeting. Adele had come in early to help him prepare coffee and set up chairs. She also brought a tin of home-baked cookies. She greeted each person who entered, then introduced people all around.

Seven other adults were seated around the table. They were already chatting about who worked where and who had been in the parish longest.

The oldest was Harold who described himself as a retired physician widower who had never had time in the past to do much volunteer work in the parish. A thirty-something man named Casey said he worked as a graphic designer, had three boys in the parish grade school, and coached soccer. Dan, an auto mechanic, was in his late forties, single, and sported a long pony tail.

"I've been on the liturgy committee for about five years now," Dan said.

Bill had come in response to a notice Nate had put in the bulletin because he "liked to keep abreast of things that are going on around here."

Bill's wife Janet toted a thick looseleaf binder. "I never miss a chance to get new volunteers involved in the festival," she said.

As the meeting was about to begin, a woman in her mid-thirties rushed through the door, a curly-haired toddler tucked under one arm, a bag filled with Cheerios, and toys and picture books hanging from the other. Bill frowned but Janet moved her chair to make more room at one corner of the table.

"I hope I'm not late," the woman said. "My husband was supposed to be home in time to take care of Josh. The girls have religious ed tonight so they couldn't watch him. By the way, I'm Glenna."

"You're not late," Nate said. "We were just about to get started. I know most of you have met, but I want to be sure you all know my good friend Rosa Martinez-Cooper from Crosstown parish. She's done a lot of volunteering there and I invited her to share some of her ideas with us.

"And is this my mother, "said Rosa, patting the elderly woman at her left on the knee. "I brought Abuela because my son had to work overtime. My husband works nights and I don't like to leave her home alone."

"We're glad you're all here," Nate said. "I invited you here because Father Ralph asked me to do something about the fact that we don't have enough parish volunteers. At first I thought turning that around would be easy. Now I'm not so sure. I need some fresh input."

"What's the problem?" Dan asked.

"I've been able to identify one part of it," Nate said. "The way we do recruitment doesn't seem to be working."

"That time-and-talent sheet was developed for us by a consultant," Bill said. "It would be working if people in the parish were willing to get off their duffs and understand that we've got to make every penny count."

"I thought volunteering had something to do with a baptismal call," Casey said. "I don't know exactly what that means."

"We volunteer because we are all members of the Body of Christ," Janet said. "If one member doesn't do his part, the whole body suffers. That's what's happening here. People just don't do their part."

"I thought we were all like a big family," Glenna said. "Everyone is supposed to pitch in to make things work, but there's always going to be some who do more than others. That's the way it is in a family."

"I think of the parish as a community," Dan said, "a worshiping community where everything begins and ends with liturgy. If we put more emphasis on the liturgical aspects of parish life, we'd have no problem getting more volunteers."

"I think we're getting off the subject," Rosa said, "but I think we're getting in touch with another part of the problem. When Bill pictures the parish, he sees a well-run business. On the other hand, Glenna sees a family. Janet pictures us as the Body of Christ, and Dan sees a community that comes together for Mass. I see a community too, but I picture more of a neighborhood where everyone knows each other and helps each other out. I think those different ideas have something to do with why some people volunteer and others don't."

"So you are saying that, since we all have different images of what a parish is supposed to be, we all have different expectations of how it works, and that affects our whole notion of parish volunteering?" Nate asked.

"When the bishop was here last year he said we were all people on a pilgrimage," Harold said. "I like that image."

Janet asked, "What's your image of parish, Casey? I know you mentioned baptismal call, but I can't remember what else you said."

"I'm not sure I should even be here," Casey said. "I'm not even a Catholic. I come to Mass every week with my wife and sons, but I haven't been baptized. I've been thinking about it for years, but I haven't done it."

"Well, you *are* here," Janet said, "so you may as well give us your opinion."

Casey's Story

"Well," Casey said, "whenever I picture Catholics, I picture people in coats. In the congregation I grew up in, everyone took their coats off and hung them up in the vestibule when they came to church. Before the service, they stood around talking about what was happening in each other's lives. After the service, they had coffee and rolls and talked about the sermon. We kids went to Bible study and some groups had meetings.

"The first thing I noticed when I came to the Catholic Church with Betty, she's my wife now, was that everyone was wearing their coats. They just came in to where the Mass was going to be and sat down. Hardly anyone talked to anyone, maybe except for their own family in the pew. They left their coats on the whole time.

"We've been here seven years now and I've gotten to know some of the people here well. They're great people but, when they come to Mass, most everyone seems to want to get in and out in a hurry. I guess that's why you all always keep on your coats. I can see why it's hard to get enough volunteers."

Imagining "Parish"

Images have a lot to do with how well things are understood and how well things work in a parish. When people working on a common task share a common image of parish, the work tends to go more smoothly than it does when they come to the work with different images. They tend to have similar ideas about how the organization at its best *should* work and similar expectations about what the results should look like.

Images help people link experience with vision and make meanings clearer by tapping into common memories and feelings. Jesus, for example, used the image of "the reign of God" to describe the world he envisioned to people who had real experience being governed by kings and emperors.

"Ideas about organization are always based on implicit images or metaphors that persuade us to see, understand, and manage situations in a particular way," writes Gareth Morgan.

Each person at Nate's meeting had zeroed in on one image that created insight into "parish." Yet, since each had selected a different image, each was likely to understand and be "parish" in different ways.

"But [images] also distort," continues Gareth Morgan. "They have strengths. But they also have limitations. In creating ways of seeing, they create ways of not seeing."

Father Ralph, for example, used an image when he first directed Nate to "beef up" the volunteer program. In working out a vision and purpose for parish-centered volunteer ministry, however, Deacon Morgan has already realized that his task extends beyond the image in Father Ralph's directive. Rather than simply recruiting enough warm bodies to flesh out the thin spots on the roster of parish volunteers, Nate will have to guide parishioners to a new understanding of what it means to be "parish" in the twenty-first century and what role parish-centered volunteers play in helping that parish move into its vision.

The images with which people are most comfortable change over time. Some are bound to work better than others. People who manage volunteers may have to experiment and use one image to help explain another.

When Jesus used "the reign of God" as an image for his vision for the world, what he was describing was very different from the real experience of his listeners. Using images helped them understand the difference. "The reign of God is like a mustard seed…," "The reign of God is like yeast…," "The reign of God is like a buried treasure…" are all images Jesus is reported to have used.

Jesus also used stories to help people understand their relationship to the reign of God. Stories have considerably more impact than simple statements of belief or opinion and can strengthen the effect of an image.

When Casey described the parish as "people with coats," the mental picture he created was clear. But his story strengthened the image's effect and helped the group "re-imagine" parish in a new way. When Casey said he wasn't surprised that the parish had trouble getting volunteers, listeners got the point in ways they were not able to do when thinking of the parish as a "family," "community," "business," or "the Body of Christ."

Volunteer Ministry Planner 3: Model Hospitality

Tap Into Imagination

One of Deacon Morgan's tasks is to discover what images of parish people have in mind when they are asked to serve as volunteers. He will want to be sure that whatever images are used to generate interest match the vision and overall purpose for volunteering.

There are several ways to go about that search. Experiment with the following options and decide on the ones you would be willing to try.

- Scout out images in Scripture that Jesus was reported to have used. Which ones most match with your vision and purpose? Put the ones that are most appropriate for you in your planning notebook.
- Picture an active volunteer in your parish. Which image would most likely help that person understand the value of parish-centered volunteer ministry? Why?
- Picture an inactive parishioner who doesn't volunteer. Which image would most likely help that person understand the value of parish-centered volunteer ministry? Why?
- Learn all you can about the images and symbols of liturgy. Which ones most match your vision and purpose? Which could breathe new life into your next communication with potential volunteers? Write these choices in your planning notebook.
- Seek out engaging stories about people who volunteer. Find out what made them get and/or stay involved in parish-centered volunteering. Listen for the images they use to describe the parish, its people, and its activities. Keep a file of stories that might inspire people to get more involved. Be sure to ask for permission before you make someone's story public.

Quick Tip: In your notebook jot down core information, the Who, What, Where, When, How, and Why of stories you find interesting. No matter how meaningful the story, it's hard to pull it up from memory when you are under pressure to produce.

- Listen to the kinds of images people use in other settings. Keep those in mind that could help breathe new life into your communication with volunteers and prospective volunteers. While you don't want to pepper every communication with sports, business, or other images from popular culture, using some of them may help you connect with people who are not familiar, or are uncomfortable, with churchy jargon. List the images you wish to keep in mind in your notebook, and then share them with other volunteer managers.

"The image of us as 'people in coats' really concerns me," Janet confided to Rosa as they walked with Abuela to the parking lot. "And we think of ourselves as a welcoming parish!"

Practical Matters 3
Modeling Hospitality

If those who are recruited as volunteers experience your parish as "people with coats," you have a big obstacle to overcome. On the other hand, if from day one they experience hospitality, the door to recruiting them to volunteer ministry is wide open.

"Welcoming" practically became a parish buzzword in the 1990s. We organized newcomer gatherings for people who had recently registered, put greeters at the entrances to the worship space, and encouraged ushers to brush up on their hospitality skills. The approach had one unfortunate result, however. It allowed the rest of us to see greeters and ushers as "owning" the ministry of hospitality in our parish. That took the rest of us off the hook. We were free to continue interacting only with people we knew.

Hospitality remains one of those practices that you can't mandate or market. You can send people to workshops to learn about hospitality. You can assign a committee to design and implement a plan to increase the level of hospitality in your parish. Ultimately, though, hospitality has to be modeled by priests, council members, administrative staff, pastoral staff, and especially by people who manage parish-centered volunteers.

In fact, if you were going to create a list of qualities that were important for people who manage parish-centered volunteers to have, hospitality would rank right up at the top. Why?

Practically speaking, it is easier to recruit and retain volunteers when we extend hospitality to newcomers and to prospective and current volunteers. It's easier to get funding and support for volunteer-oriented projects when people know and like us. Meetings are more pleasant, and hospitality creates a comfortable working environment in which to make decisions and solve problems. If you are working toward a "process" approach to management, hospitality can jump-start your efforts.

But we don't *do* hospitality just to get more volunteers and keep the ones we have happy. We *live* hospitality as a natural practice of believers, extending it to new and old parishioners, visitors, friends, people who think as we do, and people who don't.

The plus is that you don't have to wait for your parish to formally invest in the practice. You can begin simply by making up your mind to "own" the practice of hospitality in whatever areas of ministry you are involved. The following are some exercises to warm you up to the process.

- Hospitality is often understood as extending courtesies to people who share our space. But it's more than that. Genuine hospitality uses sensual experiences to build intimacy among people who share a space. Any interior designer or restaurant owner will tell you that the more you involve all five of people's senses, the more likely they are to experience you and the environment in which they engage you in a positive way.

Our homes are filled with things that help us engage in sensual experiences. So are our sacramental liturgies. In the list that follows, check those that could help create a richer sense of hospitality among the volunteers with whom you work. Add your own ideas in your planning notebook.

_____ aroma of bread, freshly baked
_____ taste of fine wine or good coffee
_____ flicker of burning candles
_____ homemade chocolate chip cookie melting in your mouth
_____ sound of music or flowing water when you enter a room
_____ aroma of a scented candle or potpourri
_____ feel of warm handshake or hug
_____ sight of a bright smile
_____ sound of a friendly voice
_____ sight of a colorful poster
_____ freshly sharpened pencils and crisp white paper
_____ other: _____

- The tone for hospitality is often expressed in the first few moments of an encounter. How effectively do you express instant hospitality to the volunteers you manage? Check the item in each pair below that most closely describes you.

When folks come to meetings, I:

_____ warmly welcome each person each time.
_____ extend a general welcome when the meeting begins.

If I'm not there when a volunteer arrives for an assignment, I:

_____ leave a note of welcome.
_____ say, "That's OK, she will know what to do."

When volunteers come to work at our parish, they:

_____ have a safe designated place to put their coats and belongings.
_____ stash coats and belongings wherever they can find a place to put them.

I make sure that, nearly every time they come to help, volunteers can enjoy:

_____ music, fresh flowers, juice, coffee, cookies, fruit, or some other treat.
_____ their work. They didn't come here to eat!

I make sure that supply storage is:

_____ clearly labeled and accessible.
_____ around somewhere. They don't mind hunting for what they need.

When volunteers want to chat, I:

_____ express genuine interest in whatever they talk about.
_____ cut them short. They have no idea how much work I have to do.

Many of us carry internal roadblocks that keep us from extending hospitality to people we don't already know. Those same roadblocks can also prevent us from being effective at recruiting and retaining parish-centered volunteers. Below is a list of possible roadblocks. Check any that apply to you.

❑ I hear "don't talk to strangers" messages from the past.
❑ I hear "don't speak until spoken to" messages from the past.
❑ No one else is introducing themselves or asking names.
❑ We've never done that kind of thing when people came to Mass or meetings.
❑ It's too much trouble to start a conversation with someone I don't know.
❑ Talking to someone new always makes me feel uncomfortable.
❑ I'd feel silly just starting up a conversation with someone I don't know.
❑ What if they are put off by my approach?
❑ We already have people who are supposed to be doing that.
❑ I really don't need any more friends.
❑ He/she wouldn't want to get to know me.
❑ If he/she really got to know me, she wouldn't like me.
❑ I don't have time to talk. My spouse/kids are in a hurry.
❑ I can never seem to remember people's names anyway.
❑ Other:_____

- Am I willing to eliminate one of these roadblocks? Which one? How? Record your plan in your notebook.

Quick Tip: In most cases, just becoming willing to change is enough to put the process in motion. Accept how you currently are. Envision how you want to be. Become willing to change. With the Holy Spirit guiding, you will discover dozens of opportunities to practice your new way of being.

Micro-Perspective

What's involved in hospitality? For most of us, it involves making the choice to extend a sense of genuine warmth, a reaching-out in a way that is meaningful to the receiver of our hospitality, a sense of personal investment in the relationship.

- Think about a specific person who volunteers in your parish or group. What one act of hospitality might make a real difference to that person? Will you choose to do it? When? Record your commitment in your planning notebook.
- Think about a specific person who does not volunteer in your parish. What one act of hospitality might make a difference to that person? Will you choose to do it? When? Record your commitment in your planning notebook.
- Picture the place where you most often meet with the volunteers you manage. What single enhancement could you bring to that space to increase the sense of hospitality there? Will you choose to bring it? When? Record your commitment in your planning notebook.

Quick Tip: In parish life, hospitality brings the sensual to the spiritual, a sense of hearth and home to a brick and mortar gathering space. Just as we fill our homes with sights, sounds, tastes, smells, and touches to nourish our spirits, our sacramental liturgies are filled with symbols and images that link the sensual with the spiritual, creating a warm and welcoming household for the people of God. Let go of that ho-hum image of "people with coats." Spread hospitality. Let people know that in *this* parish (or at least in this office or this meeting), they're going to find a fire-filled place where energy flows, interesting things happen, and life changes!

CHAPTER 4

Upper Roommates

Though Adele was out of town visiting her grandchildren, everyone else was back for the autumn meeting except for Casey who was coaching soccer and had called to say he would be late. This time Glenna came without Joshua Alexander. Janet arrived with copies of a report she wanted to share with the group. Developed by the local volunteer center, it included the most common reasons people gave for volunteering:

- to meet people
- to get out of the house
- to fill free time
- to help someone
- to have fun
- to use some currently underused skill
- to create a better world
- to not feel guilty
- to change things

- to be in charge of something
- to prepare for a career in a new field
- to flesh out a resumé
- to be part of something
- because it's expected by boss, family, friend, group
- to spend more time with family or friend
- to give back for all that's been given

Quick Tip: Your local volunteer center may have an extensive library of print and video resources. Call them to set up a visit. Another great information resource is the Association for Volunteer Administration. Visit their website, www.avaintl.org. Another useful website is www.energizeinc.com. Both include articles, resources, idea exchanges, and links to other relevant websites.

"There's nothing on that list that we haven't heard before," Bill said.

"I just thought it might help to have this on hand when we start talking about recruitment," Janet responded.

"Nearly all of them apply to me except for the one about filling free time," Glenna said with a laugh.

"Frankly, I think the only good reason on the list is one about giving back for all we've been given," Bill said. "That's what stewardship is all about."

"But it leaves a lot of people out," Rosa said. "Not everyone has time to do things for the parish. And most people think they don't have any talents the parish can use."

"That's how I felt a few years ago," Dan said. "I didn't think I had anything to offer. I didn't know enough to teach religious education. I don't like festivals, and I sure didn't feel qualified to make decisions on the parish council."

"So do you do any volunteering here?" Harold asked.

"Now I do," Dan said. "I'm on the liturgy preparation team and I teach fourth grade religious ed."

"How did that come about?" Nate asked.

Dan's Story

"I had just finished working on a car and realized that the Saturday evening Mass would begin in ten minutes. I had two choices. I could go to Mass as I was, grease and all, or I could wait till morning which I didn't want to do because I had promised friends who live ninety miles away that I would meet them for an early lunch. So I washed my hands and drove over here to church. I noticed there was a grease stain on my jacket as I slid into a side pew near the rear door just as Father Ralph was getting ready to come in.

"He tapped me on the shoulder and asked if I had ever been an altar boy. I told him I had, of course, a long time ago. So he said, 'Come on up with me. Our acolyte didn't show and I really like to have someone else up there.'

"I was embarrassed. I told him I wasn't dressed properly—that I probably looked like I'd slept in the street. He said, 'God doesn't care,' and, before I knew it, I was at the altar.

"At first I felt like everyone was staring at the grease on my jacket. Then I got caught up in what was happening. I listened closely to the readings and, now that I could see everyone sitting out there, some things seemed to click. Later Father Ralph thanked me for helping out. I told him I'd enjoyed the experience, that it made me want to learn more about the Mass, though I didn't understand why. He suggested I get in touch with the chairperson of the liturgy committee. I did. Now I can't imagine my life without being part of that team."

"I'm trying to figure out where you would fit on this list of reasons, Dan," Janet said. "What you are describing seems different."

"I agree," said Rosa. "There are lots of organizations out there who do lots of good things. People could volunteer in any of them. What we have to ask ourselves is what makes us different. Why do people choose to volunteer in this one?"

"Any one of those reasons could apply," Bill said.

"True, but I think it's something more," Harold said. "I think it's because we expect to find Christ here. I know I do."

Volunteer Ministry Planner 4: Step Up to Discipleship

Nate's group has already considered three essential components of successful parish-centered volunteer ministry:

- a common vision of how volunteering helps create a thriving parish
- a clear sense of purpose for parish-centered volunteer ministry
- willingness to model hospitality.

The fourth component is: seeing each person as a disciple of Christ. We have to be careful not to let people settle into a sort of buzzword interpretation when we use words like "disciple of Christ." If people in your parish picture either a faceless follower, passively nodding yes to everything Christ said and did, or a passionate martyr literally burning with zeal, it will be understandably difficult for them to welcome the experience of discipleship into their own lives.

As someone who manages parish-centered volunteers, your role is to draw them ever more deeply into an authentic experience of discipleship. The word "disciple" comes from a Latin root that means "to learn." Jesuit J. J. Mueller, associate professor of Theological Studies at Saint Louis University lists eight themes of discipleship in his 1992 book *Practical Discipleship: A United States Christology* (Mueller, p. 37):

- the kingdom of God present in our midst—what Jesus preached about instead of preaching about himself
- the command to love God and neighbor—our only obligation in this kingdom
- conversion—recognizing and turning away from obstacles to loving
- salvation for all—the message sent from God the Father through Jesus
- mission—the invitation to proclaim Christ's message of service to others

- the binding together of broken lives—forgiveness and reconciliation
- accepting the invitation to follow Jesus
- sharing in common discipleship through the guidance of the Holy Spirit

Aware of it or not, people who volunteer in their parishes do so because they have already experienced or are seeking one or more of the themes of discipleship in their own lives. People who want to manage parish-centered volunteers successfully will strive to sustain a parish culture where discipleship themes dominate.

This effort at discipleship is not as easy as it sounds. Because marketplace demands are so complex today, nearly every organization struggles to stay focused on its mission. Consider this example from the for-profit world.

An old, respected pharmaceutical firm defined its mission as developing new products to enhance human health. Designed to support research, testing, and reporting, and to establish solid relationships with foundations, healthcare providers, and government agencies with healthcare priorities, the bulk of its time, space, financial, and human resources are assigned to those core activities or practices.

To stay competitive, this company shifts its resources toward becoming more effective in bringing its own products to the marketplace. It adds marketing, packaging, and more to its practices. Consequently, its time, space, financial, and human resources are assigned to marketing, promotion, packaging, selling, building relationships with labs, direct healthcare providers, and consumers. If this company is not careful, the balance will shift away from the core practices that supported its original mission. Eventually, the mission becomes an afterthought as new practices begin to drive the organization.

In parish life, the same thing can happen. The core practices of parish life—celebrating, proclaiming, serving, healing, and leading—are our most important work. Guided by those core practices, we create and sustain an organization where the Holy Spirit can work. No matter how Spirit-driven our intentions, however, the enormous marketplace-driven demands some projects place on parish resources are likely to upset the balance.

An extensive building program, for example, can take on a whole life of its own consuming the bulk of the parish's time, space, financial, and human resources for several years. Though the mission and the commitment to that mission doesn't change, we begin to reassign resources to sustaining our buildings, our programs, our projects. We recruit more and more volunteers whose talents support eliminating debt, raising the most dollars, signing up the most people, designing the most interesting programs, improving the school, and boosting athletic programs over those whose goal is to take the next steps on their faith journeys. Eventually, the parish seems more driven by a marketplace model of parish life than by its original mission.

Ask volunteers what work they are doing in the parish and most will answer helping out in the school, working at a booth at the festival, and so on. It's not easy for volunteers to see their work as mission-driven because the greatest percentage of work we assign to them seems several steps removed from the real work of the parish.

Managing from the perspective of discipleship matches well with the "process" approach likely to be essential in the twenty-first century. But it also creates three unique challenges.

- *For many, "signing up" as a volunteer would be seen as a willingness to enter more fully into the experience of discipleship.* People would need to be nurtured through that experience as they risk becoming more aware of each of those themes operating more intensely in their lives. The person who manages those volunteers would be entrusted with sustaining an environment where that nurturing could happen.
- *The more deeply God's people who volunteer experience discipleship, the more powerfully they would be driven to give testimony through service in the world.* Those who manage parish volunteers would have to be interested not only in helping people discover a call to service *within* the parish but with helping people move beyond parish boundaries to bring Christ's love to an ever-widening world. That would require not only letting the most competent volunteers become interested in other areas of parish life, but encouraging them to do so.

  There are jobs to be done within the parish. But there is considerably more work to be done in the world. A truly effective parish-centered volunteer ministry will have most of its people sharing their gifts "out there." Rather than being the primary consumer of volunteers' gifts, the parish becomes the center that develops and sustains God's people for ministry in the world. It acts as if it means it when it says, "Go forth!" Rather than rituals of obligation, the celebrations its community shares truly do become the liturgical link to life.
- *Finally, what applies to God's people would also apply to the parish as a whole.* The organization itself would embrace discipleship and become what Peter Senge described in his 1992 book *The Fifth Discipline* as a "learning organization."

  Like "disciple," the word "discipline" comes from the root that means "to learn." Rather than understand this word as some sort of rigid way of doing something, Senge focuses on the meaning of "discipline" as a lifelong program of study and practice that involves exploration that results in change. This approach was difficult to implement because people had been taught to mistrust their own learning processes and had become used to expecting answers that had been proven right through research or handed down from experts and authorities.

Senge suggested five lifelong programs of study and practice:

* *personal mastery* through which we learn to expand our capacity to create the results we most desire; creating an organizational environment that encourages individuals to achieve desired goals and purposes
* *mental models* through which we reflect on our internal pictures of the world and see how they shape our actions and decisions
* *shared vision* through which we develop shared images that build a sense of commitment within a group
* *team learning* through which collective thinking skills are transformed in order to develop a group intelligence and versatility greater than the sum of individual talents
* *systems thinking* through which we see how to change systems more effectively to act more in tune with the larger processes of the natural and economic world

Though they don't use religious language, Senge's five programs for learning organizations are not all that different from Mueller's themes for individual discipleship. Both carry a sense that good comes from shared vision and images, movement toward mission-oriented results; both see value in working together for conversion and transformation. Senge's emphasis on systems thinking seems to align well with Mueller's eighth theme—sharing in common discipleship through the guidance of the Holy Spirit.

That theme of sharing in common discipleship often loses something when we try to explain it in the context of parish life. Too often it comes out sounding like "therefore you should help your parish," a conclusion that is not broad enough.

As God's people coming together in a parish, we intentionally walk with each other up this path of discipleship. We remain open to changing who does what, when, and how. Accepting our role as disciples means that, as individuals and as an organization, we agree to remain teachable. As volunteers we seek out experiences that provide opportunities for us to learn. As someone who manages volunteers, we strive to sustain an environment in which that learning can happen.

For a parish to do that, however, may mean moving away from some of what we do in response to demands of the marketplace. That feels risky, at least as risky as stepping out of that upper room must have felt to Christ's early disciples. On the one hand, people might not understand, might even be angry, if we change something that means a great deal to them. We might lose members; we might lose money. We might even fail, especially in our early efforts.

Yet change, learning to change, expecting change, embracing change has always been at the center of parish life.

"Transformation is why we gather at the Lord's table," said Donald W. Trautman, bishop of the diocese of Erie, Pennsylvania. "We are not working simply to improve liturgical ceremonies; we are working for transformation, conversion."

Managing a volunteer with the focus on discipleship doesn't just result in different answers, it raises different questions. Instead of asking, "what volunteers do we need to make our projects successful?" managers ask, "What do God's people here need to do now to learn more about what it means to follow Christ?"

- At this time, what might people in your parish need to do to learn more about what it means to follow Christ? List these learning needs in your planning book.
- How can these needs be met through the experience of volunteering?
- You may or may not be in a position from which you can influence your parish to become a "learning organization" but you can influence whether or not parish-centered volunteer ministry functions as a "learning" group. Below is a list of key characteristics of a successful learning groups. Code each description to indicate how you manage parish-centered volunteers. Use these two codes:

DTW: Do This Well   NI: Needs Improvement

_____ I frequently question assumptions about volunteering.
_____ I readily share information with anyone who is interested.
_____ I make sure people know how their work is linked to that of the parish as a whole.
_____ I redesign structures to match work processes.
_____ I'm willing to take risks.
_____ I promote collaboration.
_____ I often look to other fields for ideas and answers.
_____ I try to identify areas that could benefit from organizational healing.
_____ I encourage learning in others.
_____ I keep on learning myself.

Micro-Perspective

- Call to mind the name of the person who is a regular volunteer. If you chose to adopt one of the above characteristics, which choice would most benefit that volunteer?

- Call to mind the name of the person you envisioned who was not currently volunteering. If you chose to adapt in one of the above areas, which choice might benefit that person?

- In your opinion, if you chose to improve in one of the above areas, which choice would most benefit parish-centered volunteering overall?

- Choose one area in which you hope to improve over the next several months. Keep that area in mind as you continue to plan. Write your method for achieving this goal in your planning notebook.

- Which of the following learning opportunities are currently taking place in your parish in which volunteers can participate?

  ❑ liturgical celebrations
  ❑ small faith-sharing groups
  ❑ Scripture study
  ❑ days of reflection
  ❑ parish retreats
  ❑ adult education classes
  ❑ cross-cultural experiences
  ❑ leadership development workshops
  ❑ study groups for people in specific areas of service
  ❑ field trips
  ❑ support groups
  ❑ brainstorming sessions
  ❑ "values" discussions
  ❑ ministry-specific trainings
  ❑ other: _____

- If you could add one more opportunity from the list above to what the parish is already offering, what would it be? Record your choice in your planning folder.

- Brainstorm ways to make existing opportunities more oriented to "learning." Add your ideas to the list below. (Hint: Think of unlikely combinations. Volunteers often learn one area of parish-centered ministry well and neglect others.)

- ❑ game day for catechists
- ❑ social justice study group for volunteers in liturgical ministries
- ❑ field trip to a low income parish for members of the stewardship or finance committee
- ❑ support group for people who work with human concerns
- ❑ _____
- ❑ _____
- ❑ _____

■ Review your vision and purpose statements for parish-centered volunteer ministry. In light of what you have been reading and thinking, do you want to add, delete, or change either of them? If so, write your revised statements in your planning notebook.

$$\sim$$

Deacon Morgan couldn't believe that he was thinking of abandoning the traditional time/talent sign-up form. What he had in mind instead was sort of a wish/wonder form that would look something like this:

NAME: _____ PHONE: _____

ADDRESS: _____

BEST TIME TO CALL: _____

I would describe myself as...

outgoing	prayerful	introspective
hospitable	artistic	creative
organized	optimistic	business-like
a friend to all	studious	serious
thrifty	energetic	a good leader
a good teacher	a good role model	a good planner
an animal lover	kind	a peace-maker
stickler for detail	persistent	an organizer
blessed with a great sense of humor		
other:_____		

I wish I were more...

_____

_____

Five things I really enjoy doing are:

planning	working with people	singing
coming to Mass	listening to stories	telling/reading stories
cooking	gardening	writing letters
talking on the phone	public speaking	going on outings
other:_____		

I wish I knew more about…

Scripture	liturgy	religious teachings
how to help the homeless	children	teenagers
marriage	making bread	singing
carpentry	gardening	speaking Spanish
budgeting	how the parish works	having fun
desktop publishing	drawing/painting	planning events
how to make things happen	justice issues	Church history
how the parish works		
other:_____		

The more Nate considered the idea, the more he realized that it raised a whole different way of looking at parish volunteering. If people saw volunteering as a way to learn something they didn't already know, they might feel less pressure to perform whatever the task might be perfectly. They might also be willing to get involved with something as a project rather than thinking they had to make a commitment for a year or more.

When he ran the idea of a wish/wonder sign-up process past Marge in the office, she couldn't believe it either.

"That's an interesting suggestion," Marge said politely. "But it's just not practical. First of all, no one will answer the questions. They're personal. And they don't seem to have a lot to do with church. Second, how would we handle the information when we got it? The answers could go all over the map. Our database isn't set up that way. Last but not least, what would we do with the information if we could key it in somehow? What good would it do a committee chair to know that Joe Smith wants to learn more about Scripture?"

"So you really like the idea," Nate teased.

"Morgan, if you do something like this, people will think we've lost our minds over here. That phone is going to ring off the hook. And I'm going to forward every one of those calls to your office!"

Practical Matters 4

React to a Risky Idea

Check which of the following statements that best expresses your reaction to Deacon Morgan's idea:

- ❏ It's ridiculous and impractical.
- ❏ It's so crazy, it just might work.
- ❏ It probably won't work, but it's worth a try.
- ❏ I like it, but it would never fly in our parish.
- ❏ I'm skeptical, but keeping an open mind.
- ❏ I can see how it might work well with certain people or in certain situations.
- ❏ What a great idea! I'm willing to try it out.
- ❏ It's a bit of a risk, but an idea like this could really move us closer to our goals.
- ❏ Let's go for it!

Deacon Morgan's wish/wonder approach is only one of many ways to draw people more fully into the experience of discipleship through volunteering. Keep it in mind as a reminder that managers in learning organizations frequently challenge their assumptions about how things should be done. They also risk trying something new when they can see that the approach would be more in line with the organization's mission.

- ■ Before you plan your next effort to recruit parish volunteers, resolve to challenge your own assumptions. When new ideas arise, use this list to monitor your reaction. Ask yourself what it would take to allow you to make the next step toward accepting this idea. What would it take to get you to try a different way of recruiting volunteers? Check all that apply.

_____ approval from a particular manager
_____ a bigger budget
_____ strong support from the pastor or others in authority
_____ more confidence in my own ability
_____ absolute certainty that the idea will work
_____ extra help
_____ other: _____

Fear-Busters

Sometimes, what holds us back from trying something new is our fear of how we'll be seen by others. The call to discipleship starts with learning something new, and then requires us to act on what we learn. When someone presents a new idea, it's not uncommon for those who can carry it out to wait until just about everyone in the parish nods in approval. For an organization that claims to be open to the work of the Holy Spirit within it, we sometimes seem almost paralyzed to move out of our comfort zone.

> Quick Tip: This might be a good time to read Luke 6:17–26.

- Want to deal with the fear? Start with the first question below. When you can answer yes, move on to the next question. As you move through the list, your confidence level will grow. You won't be eliminating the risk, but you will be increasing your ability to deal with whatever happens.

- Will taking this action move us closer to our vision for the parish?
- If trying this idea is successful, will it help us more effectively fulfill our purpose?
- Does it match with our current and long-term priorities?
- Have we done our homework?
- Do the potential rewards outweigh potential losses?
- Am I (are we) willing to accept responsibility for either its success or failure?
- Can we find the resources we need to carry it out?
- Does it feel right at "gut level"?

Banish Budget Blues

Would you like to send the human concerns committee to a conference, but can't ask them to pay from their own pockets? Do you think a day of reflection is a great idea, but there's no money to pay for it? Are you of the opinion that the entire stewardship committee should read a book, but can't foot the bill for a dozen copies?

Before you do another thing in planning for parish-centered volunteer ministry, find out when budgets are prepared in your parish. Take a look at last year's budget. You are likely to find allocations for salaries, capital improvements, repairs, supplies, educational materials, programs, outreach, printing, interest payments, insurance, even light bulbs, and a whole lot more. What you are not likely to find are items related to expenses for recruiting and developing volunteers.

- Think realistically about what you will need to best serve the volunteers whose work you manage. Check those that apply.

    ❑ registration fees for an upcoming conference?
    ❑ tuition money for a relevant class?
    ❑ funds for a day off-site, reflecting and planning?
    ❑ relevant books to study and spark new ideas?
    ❑ start-up funds to launch a new project?
    ❑ petty cash for unexpected expenses?
    ❑ decorating dollars to spruce up the room where volunteers meet?
    ❑ design, editing, and printing fees for a quarterly volunteer-oriented newsletter?

It's OK to submit new budget requests not just for what programming needs to survive, but for what the volunteers who make those programs need to thrive.

Will you get the money the first time you ask for it? Maybe not. But you will raise awareness in your budget committee and parish council. You may even be given the opportunity to speak about the bottom-line value volunteers add to parish ministries.

> Quick Tip: At last reckoning, volunteer hours for typical parish work would be billed out to professionals at an average cost of $17.42 per hour. Much of the work would be billed out at a considerably higher rate. Do the math. If your parish only uses 200 volunteer hours a month, it receives more than $40,000 in added value from their work.

If you are persistent, your parish may begin to look at the entire budget in a different way. In the meantime, the volunteers you manage will begin to appreciate how important their work is in fulfilling the mission of the parish.

CHAPTER 5

Sparks!

B ill had been grumbling for the better part of the year that the group wasn't moving fast enough. He had wanted to do a volunteer recruitment drive in April, adding that, while Pentecost made sense liturgically, it had never been his first choice of a date because some folks had already left for summer vacations.

But Bill had been overruled. Immersed in study about the themes of discipleship, the group decided to wait. Even Janet sided with the majority, though she did ask Casey to help her create a rather catchy poster and flyer to invite people to work at the festival. The rest of the group agreed to each introduce themselves to ten people they didn't know, learn their names, and invite them face to face to help out at the festival. The simple approach had been amazingly successful. Many of the folks who were asked brought spouses or friends to the orientation meeting Janet scheduled. Still, in Bill's opinion, that wasn't much to show for a year's worth of work.

Worse, he was getting tired of having to deal with the extra people who weren't even supposed to be at their meetings. Rosa's mother, for one. Nate had found a threadbare recliner that was comfortable enough for Abuela to doze off in and Abuela actually snored through one of Bill's best suggestions.

In fact, Rosa wasn't even supposed to be there. She belonged to Crosstown parish and almost always brought friends from that parish with her to the meetings. Collaborating or not, Bill didn't see how anyone else should have a say in what happened at Saints Alive.

The final straw was that boy, however. Glenna had brought him to almost every meeting. Now that he was three, he talked incessantly while he played and often interrupted Glenna while she tried to participate in the meeting. Once he'd spilled juice on the table and, sure enough, he had juice with him again tonight.

Glenna had also brought a young woman with her. "Cheryl and her husband Doug moved in next-door in September," Glenna explained. "You're going to want to hear what happened when they joined the parish."

Cheryl's Story

"Six years ago Doug and I got engaged. We hadn't been regular churchgoers in college, but when we decided to marry, we agreed it was time to join a parish. We weren't just looking for a place to get married, we really intended to get involved," Cheryl said.

"My apartment was nearby so we came here to register. The priest had us fill out several forms. He told us about Mass times and described dozens of activities. We toured the parish buildings and saw plans for the new school wing.

"Back in his office he told us how much we were expected to contribute, handed us brochures about the parish and a folder about planning Catholic weddings, and said someone would call to sign us up for one of the volunteer ministries. No one ever called but, if they had, we wouldn't have signed up for anything."

"Why not?" Janet asked.

"The priest was really nice, and he gave us a lot of information," Cheryl said. "But even during the pre-wedding meetings, he didn't seem all that interested in *us*, as if all that was important was what was expected *from* us. He only talked about the school and the buildings and how much money it took to run everything."

"That doesn't sound like Father Ralph," Dan said.

"It wasn't," Cheryl said. "He was the pastor before Father Ralph. Until Glenna invited me to come here tonight, no one ever asked us to get involved."

"If you are registered, you get a letter and sign-up card in the mail every year," Bill protested. "Everyone does. Don't tell me no one ever asked you to get involved."

"Bill!" Janet said.

"Well, I'm tired of excuses," Bill said. "I'm sorry, folks, but we just don't have time to talk to everyone personally. No offense, but we're all adults here and we shouldn't have to lead everybody by the hand."

"That's interesting," said Rosa. "At Crosstown, we don't have money to do parish-wide mailings, so we don't even try to run an annual recruitment drive. Even if we did, our secretary doesn't have a computer that can handle an extensive database. We have to ask people for help when we need it. We don't have as many volunteers as we need either, but just about everybody gets recruited face to face."

"When you think about it," Dan said, "if people are really expecting to find Jesus here, that seems more like the approach Jesus would have used."

Lessons From Scripture

What did Jesus know about recruiting volunteers? We can look for clues in scriptural accounts of how he approached the people who became his disciples. As we read, however, we must remember not to view Jesus as the model of factory-based management style. If we do, we're likely to see Jesus approaching prospective disciples with his divinity shining through so relentlessly that he could draw people to him effortlessly and manage them effectively with a firm but benevolent mix of command and control.

But if we see the human side of Jesus, we read a different story, that of a human Jesus trusting in a process that would come to be called discipleship. Let's start with Matthew.

> As Jesus was walking along the Sea of Galilee he watched two brothers, Simon now known as Peter and his brother Andrew, casting a net into the sea. They were fishermen. He said to them, "Come after me and I will make you fishers of men." They immediately abandoned their nets and became his followers. He walked along farther and caught sight of two other brothers, James, Zebedee's son, and his brother John. They too were in their boat getting their nets in order with their father, Zebedee. He called them, and immediately they abandoned boat and father to follow him (4:18–22).

From this passage, what can we observe about Jesus' approach?

- *He walked.* He didn't put a notice in the local bulletin and wait in an office to see if anyone responded. Instead he went prospecting.
- *He went to where overlooked prospects might be.* He didn't rely on the "usual suspects." Instead, he invested time going out into the ordinary day-to-day working world to find his recruits.
- *Their names seem important.* Though it's not reported here, it's likely one of the first things Jesus did when he met the men was find out their names. In any event, the writer thought it was important for readers to know who they were from the very first sentence.
- *He appreciated them in their own role.* The first people he reportedly found were not hanging around temple waiting for their chance to become disciples in training. They caught fish. They undoubtedly took pride in doing it well. There is no sense here that Jesus saw what they did as less holy than what he did or that what he wanted them to do was better than what they

were already doing. There were no guilt trips, no "shoulds"; just an offer of something different to do with their time.

- *He gave them a simple but intriguing job description.* Granted, it was simple: *Come follow me* was all he was asking. It was the second half of his sentence, with its air of mystery and personal challenge, that undoubtedly caught their attention.

- *He used an image with which they could identify.* Contemporary marketers do this all the time. They use images to portray speed, power, and adventure to convince folks to buy fast cars. The guys Jesus was interested in were committed to fishing. If he'd told them that by following him they would spend their time baking great loaves of bread, they would probably have said, "No thanks!"

- *He didn't expect them to recruit others.* When they responded positively, he didn't breathe a sigh of relief and say "I found you to help me, now you go find a few more people to help you." Instead, he kept on walking and prospecting.

Mark's account (Mark 1:16–20) is similar to Matthew's, but Luke has a different twist.

As he stood by the Lake of Gennesaret and the crowd pressed in on him to hear the word of God, he saw two boats moored by the side of the lake; the fishermen had disembarked and were washing their nets. He got into one of the boats, the one belonging to Simon, and asked him to pull out a short distance from the shore; then, remaining seated, he continued to teach the crowds from the boat. When he had finished speaking, he said to Simon, "Put out into deep water and lower your nets for a catch." Simon answered, "Master, we have been hard at it all night long and have caught nothing; but if you say so, I will lower the nets." Upon doing this they caught such a great number of fish that their nets were at the breaking point. They signaled to their mates in the other boat to come and help them. These came, and together they filled the two boats until they nearly sank.

At the sight of this, Simon Peter fell at the knees of Jesus saying, "Leave me Lord for I am a sinful man," for indeed, amazement at the catch they had made seized him and all his shipmates, as well as James and John, Zebedee's sons, who were partners with Simon. Jesus said to Simon, "Do not be afraid. From now on you will be catching men." With that they brought their boats to land, left everything, and became his followers (Luke 5:1–11).

In Luke's account, what approach does Jesus take?

- *He admits that he needs help and asks for it.* It's not that Jesus doesn't want to handle things by himself. He realizes that, if he is going to serve this crowd effectively, he needs something he doesn't already have. In this case, it's Simon's boat. But it isn't long before Jesus lets Simon know that it is the man himself that is needed.
- *He doesn't ask for a long-term commitment.* He doesn't ask for a lifetime or even a year's commitment up front. Instead, he asks for help on a short-term basis, with a task that is both important and do-able.
- *He involves the prospect in a hands-on demonstration.* Rather than talking his proposal, Jesus walks the fisherman through a demonstration of his hoped-for results.
- *When the prospects respond from a position of scarcity, he shows them real abundance.* No cheerleading here, no motivational speeches. Just honest conviction in miracle.
- *He sees them as worthy of high work.* Though the disciples clearly lack training for the kind of work he has in mind, Jesus doesn't protest or even say, "You'll do in spite of your faults" or "Four years of study and you'll be ready to serve." He just says, "Don't be afraid."

Can we learn anything from how Jesus called his first disciples? Today's volunteers say yes. If deep down, most people who volunteer through the parish are hoping to encounter Christ through the experience, then it makes sense to mirror Christ's way of being right from the start.

Volunteer Ministry Planner 5:
Commit to Ongoing Recruitment

■ So far, we have twelve ideas we can borrow from Jesus' approach. How might each apply to your own approach to recruiting volunteers? Consider the suggestions below. Check the ones that make sense to incorporate into recruitment plans at your parish.

❏ *We make face-to-face prospecting a priority* instead of relying on mass mailings, time/talent sheets, and notices in the bulletin.

❏ *We go to people instead of waiting for them to come to us.* We don't hound for prospects in the grocery store, but we do make the parish visible in unexpected places. We greet people sincerely when they come for Mass; we say hello and/or call them for ideas and opinions even when they haven't signed up to work on a particular committee or project.

❑ *We make a sincere effort to learn to use people's names.* Calling people by name is contagious. When you talk with uninvolved parishioners, it's not unusual to hear them say, "No one around here even knows my name."

> Hint: The solution to that is so simple. Ask! Don't be afraid. If you see them again and can't remember their name, admit it and ask again. Don't be afraid!

❑ *We picture parishioners in a wide frame.* Instead of viewing them through the straw of their involvement with parish, we appreciate the collages of their lives, the ongoing contributions they make through work, family life, hobbies, and so on. We don't presume that the work we need them to do is holier, more worthy of their time, or better that what they are already doing, just something different to do in the vast world of good work.

❑ *We present clear job descriptions that promise interesting results.* Before we ever approach prospective volunteers, we think through the specifics of what we want them to do, why it needs doing, and what will be exciting about the results.

❑ *We connect with people by using images.* We don't fill our speech and writings with churchy language for its own sake. Instead we help people connect with the parish by using creative images and stories that are meaningful to them to get our point across.

❑ *We don't expect people to recruit the rest of their team.* Too often, the first person recruited ends up being the group leader or committee chair by default. No wonder no one wants to be the first to say yes.

❑ *We admit that we are asking for help because we really need it.* Too often, people on both sides of the invitation to volunteer assume that the only reason we are turning to volunteers is because we don't have time, can't afford, or don't want to do it ourselves. When we manage in a discipleship mode, we admit that we need volunteers because they bring something to the table that we do not have. We need them because they have something real to offer.

❑ *We only ask for short-term commitments.* We allow people to tiptoe into the arena of parish-centered volunteering. We find ways to break long-term programs into shorter term projects and, when the commitment is completed, we don't expect people to stay on just because keeping them in place is easier than recruiting new volunteers.

❏ *We involve the prospect in a hands-on demonstration.* Show is always better than tell. Start FYI (For Your Inspiration) initiatives. Invite people to a meeting, activity, event, just to help them gain understanding of what the committee or group actually does. If they volunteer, great. If not, that's OK too.

❏ *When prospective volunteers respond from a position of scarcity, we show them real abundance.* Instead of lamenting over how many people aren't helping, celebrate those who are. Stress the benefits of parish-centered volunteering, rather than dire predictions of what will happen if no one helps. Don't know the benefits? Plan to start a list soon. (See chapter 7 for ideas.)

❏ *We see volunteers as worthy of important work in spite of their lack of training or understanding of church.* They may not say so, but many people don't volunteer in a parish because they see themselves as unworthy. They don't want to be stuck making coffee or sweeping out the storage closet, but they believe that low-level tasks are the only things volunteers are trusted to do. They perceive parish volunteers who get to do more meaningful things as people who know a lot about religion, or are close friends with the pastor, or even as self-righteous goody-goodies. That's not how they are and it's not how they want to be, so they stay away.

Carrying out one or more of these twelve practices may involve a significant change in how you approach recruitment for parish-centered volunteer ministry. In order to do use the ideas well, it is essential to see recruitment as more than a one-time annual appeal. Appeals may still be part of your recruitment process, but you will have more success if you put the bulk of your efforts into ongoing recruitment.

As they discussed ways to expand their thinking about recruiting volunteers, Janet was skeptical, but she agreed to think through how to incorporate some of those practices into her volunteer recruitment plans for next year's festival.

"Anyone want to help?" she asked.

"I will," Dan said.

"I thought you didn't like festivals," Harold said.

"I don't. But I have a few ideas that might help us out on the liturgy committee too," Dan said. "Besides, I'm teachable."

"Anyone else? Glenna? Rosa?"

Sure enough, just at that moment, Josh's juice spilled all over the table.

"I'd like to, but now is not a good time." Glenna seemed a bit more distracted than usual as she mopped up the spill.

"I'll help," Rosa said, "but let's meet at my home. It would be easier than bringing Abuela this way again."

Before they left for the evening, Nate handed each of them a copy of an article he'd read in a newsletter about parish management.

"Read it and see what you think," Nate said. "If you want, we can talk about it when we get together again in November.

The Story of the Future

Commitment to social justice always challenges parish leaders to take a world view, but can global issues actually affect local parish volunteers? You bet they can! While just about everyone agrees that there are no sure things as we move into the twenty-first century, those who study the future can point to worldwide changes in demographics, income distribution, education, and ways of working that are likely to have dramatic effects on every institution in the new century's first quarter.

Below are some circumstances that many agree will exist well before 2020. Some organizations are already preparing to adapt so that they can turn changes that could have negative results into positive opportunities. Volunteer parish leaders who discussed these predictions recently were surprised to discover how challenges that at first only seemed to impact people far from home might indeed have an effect on their own parishes and, ultimately, parish volunteers. Does what they had to say match with what you might experience at your parish? Could preparing for the possibilities now make parish life easier down the road? Why not gather a group of interested parishioners and talk about it!

- *Shifts in age distribution.* It's no secret that U.S. baby boomers are getting older. Nor is it news that the number of young people is growing more slowly than the number of older people. The shift in age distribution here, however, is accompanied by a rise in birthrate in underdeveloped countries, a situation that is likely to put worldwide strains on the supply of life essentials such as water, food, and clean air. Some parishes may find themselves faced with more elderly people in need and fewer young parishioners to help meet those needs. They may find themselves with increased communication challenges as they struggle to serve ever more immigrating people who speak different languages and need homes, healthcare, education, and jobs. Parish leaders see advantages in starting now to educate parishioners about justice issues and discover ways in which they might become involved in positive social action. They also see value in addressing language barriers head-on by raising volunteers' comfort levels with using other languages in liturgy, by offering adult education language classes, and by encouraging volunteers to visit nearby parishes whose membership base includes a higher percentage of Asian, African-American, and Hispanic people.

• *Shifts in distribution of income.* More Americans will have less money and the gap between the rich and the poor is likely to grow. People may need to retire later and may need to be flexible about the number of jobs they hold and the number of hours they work. By extension, parishes may feel time and money constraints. Parish leaders can meet this challenge by designing parish volunteer jobs in new ways, for example, breaking big jobs down into smaller pieces that could be handled by different volunteers. Other suggestions included recruiting volunteers for one-time projects instead of year-long commitments, hiring or appointing a volunteer coordinator, and expanding collaborative efforts with other parishes and community agencies.

• *Shifts in how to define "success."* Choosing between short-term gains and long-term prosperity will become more important. Parishes that want to thrive may have to be sure they are focusing fully on their mission, planning more carefully for the long term, and willing to risk letting go of programs and activities that no longer move their parish toward its mission (or that other groups can do more effectively). These decisions, in turn, may create a need for volunteers who can help people work through differences of opinion. The shift also calls for attention to discipleship. The need for volunteers in community agencies will be extensive; parishes may need to encourage volunteers to share their skills in new places. Those volunteers will still look to the parish for strong spiritual support, however. Designing a volunteer ministry program with plenty of spiritual dynamics built in is likely to be the most effective way to recruit, retain, and recognize parish volunteers in the new century.

Practical Matters 5

Cheryl's story highlights the fact that, whoever handles it, "registration" is a critical moment for parish-centered volunteer ministry. A one-time-contact, one-size-fits-all approach may not bring the results you want.

When Cheryl and Doug joined the parish, the priest who registered them seized on what he perceived to be a teachable moment. Unfortunately the young couple wasn't prepared to learn what he wanted to teach them. The pastor made the mistake many of us make when we try to promote something we care about with new people: we talk more about *us* than about *them*.

■ Involvement is more likely to result when we sincerely approach registration as the beginning of a long-term relationship. Consider this scenario. New neighbors have just moved in. You've gone over to welcome them. Which of the statements below would help to successfully launch the relationship? Check your choices.

_____ how often you expect them to mow their lawn
_____ what flowers you would like to see in their yard when you look out your window
_____ that you need them to pick up your mail every other weekend when you go to your cabin in the woods
_____ that you are glad they moved in and you are hoping to get to know them better

Though we may have expectations when it comes to human relationships, we understand that trust needs to develop as the relationship evolves. Why do we expect so much less from parish life?

Here is how a parish might seem to new parishioner if we allowed the relationship to evolve.

• Registration: *They seem glad to have us!*
• Plus 1 month: *Every time we come here someone new says hello!*
• Plus 3 to 6 months: *Each month I am invited to be a guest at some meeting or activity. There's no pressure to sign up.*
• Plus 6 months: *I'm getting to know several people well. I'm starting to feel at home here.*
• Plus 9 months: *So many parishioners volunteer! You gotta respect that.*
• Plus 12 months: *Someone invited me to come tonight to learn about being a lector. They said my speaking voice is a real gift!*
• Plus 12 months and three days. *How nice of the lector chairperson to call, thank me for coming, and ask if I had any questions!*
• Plus 12 months and 2 weeks: *Now I've been invited to a session where I can try lectoring out.*
• Plus 12 months and 4 weeks: *The session was wonderful and the people were really nice. There isn't time in my schedule to be a lector right now, but next fall, I am signing up!*

■ How might we adapt our parish registration process to seem more like launching a relationship? Write your thoughts in your planning notebook.

Getting the Words Right

Too often in parish life, we confuse *prospecting* with *recruitment*. Prospecting is the first step; recruitment follows. Most of the tools we currently use to recruit volunteers are actually tools that are designed to identify *prospects*. What we get when we put a notice in the bulletin, hand out a flyer, or send out a mass mailing, are names of people who are *most likely* to volunteer.

■ Think about it. What are your most common complaints about volunteers? Check the statements below that apply.

_____ They signed up but never showed up.
_____ They showed up but didn't do anything.
_____ They showed up once but never came back.
_____ They showed up but they really wanted to do something else.
_____ The same people are always the ones who volunteer.

■ What are the most common complaints you hear from people who sign up to volunteer? Check the statements below that apply.

_____ I signed up but no one ever called me.
_____ I came but they didn't have anything for me to do.
_____ I didn't realize how much of a commitment this was going to be.
_____ I thought I was supposed to do this but they expected me to do that.
_____ I came but I was the only one who didn't know anybody. I didn't fit in.

■ Many of these disappointments will be avoided when we redesign our recruitment tools with prospecting in mind. Below is a list of tools you may be using to recruit volunteers. Check the ones you used in your last recruitment drive.

_____ want ads
_____ ministry fairs
_____ educational fairs
_____ bulletin notice
_____ mass mailings/time & talent sheets
_____ targeted mailings
_____ ministry-by-ministry campaigns
_____ bulletin board ad

_____ newsletter
_____ promotional brochure
_____ witness talks after Mass
_____ open training session
_____ phone campaign
_____ invited guests to a meeting
_____ newspaper publicity
_____ other: _____

If you are like most of us, the message that came through in each of these tools was "Please sign up." In order for people to do that, they have to be willing to skip the next step: knowing what they are getting themselves into. A better message is "If we have piqued your interest, please get in touch. We have lots more information to share and we would welcome the opportunity to get to know you better." Then be sure to follow up personally and quickly with those who respond.

Here are some other ways to effectively recruit volunteers.

Stand-Up Prospecting

Sometimes opportunity knocks unexpectedly. You are introduced at a parish meeting and given a minute to say a few words. Other times, you're asked well in advance and given several minutes to report on a current project. Either situation is a prime opportunity to recruit volunteers—if you are prepared to take advantage of it. How can you make the most of those unexpected chances to expand your volunteer base?

- *Know your mission.* Be able to describe what you do in a few words. People listen when others demonstrate a sense of purpose. They may not share your passion, but they will respect you for having one.
- *Be specific.* When you start with something generic, for example, We *serve the poor,* listeners tend to start thinking in a dozen different directions. Some may tune out altogether. On the other hand, when you start with We *serve meals at the Third Street Homeless Shelter twice each month,* you help your listeners focus their interest. As a result they are more likely to listen to what you say next.
- *Tell a story.* Play down data and highlight human interest. Be prepared to talk about the people whom your project's volunteers serve. Practice telling a funny, sad, or heartwarming success story in a minute or less. Instead of saying, *Each time about twelve volunteers serve 430 meals,* try, *A really interesting thing happened on one of our visits to the shelter....*

- *Know what you need.* Now is the time to be specific. While they are still basking in the emotion of your story, spell out the critical data. For example, *We could use three more men and women on the first Tuesday of each month between 5:00 and 7:00 P.M.*
- *Be prepared to follow up.* Tell people *exactly* where they can find you during the break. Then be there. Be prepared to take their names, addresses, and phone numbers. Carry a business card with your name and number for them to take along. (Before you sit down, enthusiastically thank the meeting's chairperson for giving you the chance to ask for help.)
- *Follow up.* Within three days, phone everyone who talked with you, even if they did not decide to volunteer. If you don't get to speak with them personally, send a note. Let them know that you appreciated their interest and would like to keep in touch. Then do.

Whenever a prospect comes forward, respond immediately with your commitment to hospitality and discipleship in mind. Gwen Jackson, a lifelong church volunteer who eventually logged in over 350,000 travel miles in her role as National Chairman of Volunteers for the American Red Cross, said that managers should treat volunteers with the same respect they would show a co-worker and establish relationships with potential volunteers through ongoing hospitality. Gwen's recommendations?

- *Use a person's name whenever you talk with them.* It lets them know that you value them as an individual, not just because they happen to be part of a committee or work group.
- *Ask for suggestions about programs you are working on.* Don't rely on evaluation sheets after the fact. If someone shows an interest in your project, tell them what you are planning and ask for opinions. Next time a similar project rolls around, they will be more likely to say yes when you invite them to help.
- *Thank people for their comments.* If you are talking face to face, thank them right away. But if they drop you a note or leave a voice-mail or e-mail message, get back to them as soon as possible to let them know how much you appreciate their support.
- *Praise your current volunteers.* Letting people know how much you appreciate volunteers efforts tells them that, if they volunteer in the future, they won't go unnoticed.
- *Make it easy for prospective volunteers to reach you.* Use posters, parish bulletin and other communication pieces to let people know that new volunteers

are always welcome. Be sure to include the phone number of a contact person.

- *Say hello to strangers.* Take Gwen's advice and reach out to people you don't know yet. Even people who come to Mass regularly say that there are more people than ever there whom they haven't met. Take the initiative. Start introducing yourself to strangers. You may be surprised at the wealth of potential you discover.

Designing a Prospecting Tool

Keep in mind that no ad, notice, announcement, mailing, or any other tool is a substitute for face-to-face contact. The tools do serve an important purpose, however, in raising awareness about the presence and value of parish-centered volunteer ministry. The list that follows is an overview of the key elements of a successful prospecting tool. Now take a look at one of the tools you used recently in your parish. Check off how many key elements are present.

_____ includes a vision of how the parish looks different as a result of thriving volunteer ministry

_____ includes a clear sense of purpose for parish-centered volunteer ministry

_____ uses images and/or stories that link with people's perception of "parish"

_____ expresses sincere hospitality

_____ promotes volunteering as a learning process

_____ strengthens the sense of relationship

_____ acknowledges the value of all that people do as volunteers outside of the parish

_____ tells the truth about what is needed

_____ gives clear directions about how and to whom to respond

_____ gives clear information about how and who will follow up

_____ is fun to read, hear, or experience

We will spend more time working on prospecting tools in later chapters. For now, answer the following questions. If we could select just one element from the list above to improve the prospecting tool we used recently, what would it be? How could we incorporate that element most effectively? Write your responses in your planning notebook.

CHAPTER 6

It's a Match!

For the next meeting, Nate invited the local volunteer center director to talk with the group about managing volunteers. As an afterthought, he'd sent an open invitation to four nearby parishes and about twenty new people had come. Afterwards, the director led them in a discussion of the article Nate handed out at the last meeting. She also told them about community-based study groups forming at the local library to learn more about global issues.

Harold latched on to this idea and, in front of everyone, he asked Adele to accompany him to the next library study group. Harold was visibly pleased when she agreed. Then he volunteered to write a short summary of the global issues forums and send copies to each parish. Harold was an excellent reporter and a good writer. Soon, his lively monthly summaries were appearing in bulletins in five area parishes.

Even though winter weather forced a number of building closures and meeting cancellations, the group had managed to develop a pilot plan for ongoing volunteer recruitment. Two committee chairs were already testing it out. Janet decided to personally introduce herself to two people she didn't know each weekend and invite them to help at the Summer Festival. If only one agreed, she reasoned, there would still be at least eighteen new people involved this year.

Dan launched what he called his "invite three" initiative and personally invited three new people to help prepare liturgy for the Easter season. Two had come and one, Susan, agreed to join the liturgy committee. Planning for Ordinary Time would begin next month. Susan was bringing a friend and Dan had repeated his "invite three initiative." This time all three had agreed to give liturgy preparation a try.

"With several newcomers on board, we're going to start a little study group to help everyone learn more about why we do what we do in liturgy," Dan said. "Folks from your parish are more than welcome to come, Rosa."

The group's next step was to pilot-plan a matching process. Cheryl reminded the group that the director of the volunteer center had encouraged them to offer volunteers interesting short-term projects instead of asking them to do repetitive work with long-term commitments.

"Picture this," Cheryl said. "You work at a job you love. Lately, though, you feel you could be doing more. You are longing for something that will challenge you to grow. Monday, your boss says 'I have two projects that need doing. Choose the one you want. I'll assign the other one to Tom.'"

"That would never happen at our company," Casey said. "They just hand us a project and say 'we needed this yesterday!'"

"Bear with me," said Cheryl. "Project A is routine. Won't take any time at all. Project B is a bit of a challenge. You might have to stretch a little, but you are guaranteed to learn something. And the project is truly meaningful. It's likely to make a difference in helping your company reach its goals. Which would you choose?"

"Project B, definitely," said Casey. "Why would you work on something that didn't matter?"

"I don't know," Glenna said. Joshua was playing quietly for once, arranging a plastic barn and farm animal set on an empty bookshelf. "What if you were really busy with other projects? Wouldn't you be better off choosing the easy one?"

"Maybe," said Rosa. "It would all depend on your motivation, what you wanted to get out of the job."

"If you want to get anywhere, you'd be better off choosing B and making time for it," Bill said. "Especially if you need to impress your boss."

"That's probably true, Bill," said Dan, "but if it meant I couldn't do my other work well, I'd still choose A. On the other hand, I'd choose B if I could make time for it and I wouldn't choose it to impress my boss. I'd choose it for me. For the satisfaction I would get out of it."

"Was that the point you were trying to make, Cheryl?" Nate asked.

"Part of it," Cheryl said. "But everybody's answer makes sense, don't you think? My point was that people choose work projects for different reasons. If we are going to be effective in recruiting volunteers, especially if we are going to work from a discipleship model, we're going to have to take all of those reasons into account, be flexible in designing volunteer jobs, and really be clear about expectations on both sides. I think that's what the volunteer center director meant when she told us we needed to think about matching."

Matching People With Work

When a job arises that can be filled by a parish volunteer, think of yourself as a matchmaker. Bypass the "any warm body will do" approach and try instead to find a good match. The person who volunteers will be happier and the job is more likely to be done well.

Traditional time/talent forms can help potential volunteers select committees or activities that sound appealing. But they can't tell the volunteer what a commitment to that activity really includes, and they can't say anything specific about the level of interest and skill a potential volunteer brings. Experienced volunteer managers agree that designing short-term projects, clear job and project descriptions, and personal interviews are much more reliable tools.

Designing Jobs as Projects

Today's volunteers are often reluctant to make long-term commitments to committee work but will happily accept short-term or one-time projects. Dan is now using a project approach with the liturgy committee, asking for help for just one liturgical season. This year, the team preparing for the Easter season will work together January through April. Advent and Christmas season teams start planning in September, and preparations for the season of Lent begins in November. His "invite three" initiative ensures that new members will always be learning about liturgical preparation, quickly becoming real contributors to one or more seasons' planning. Even if they don't come back to help with the following season, they are likely to be more fully invested in the parish's worship life.

Nearly every parish group can benefit from considering a redesign of their work processes. Instead of recruiting catechists to teach fourth grade in the style of a self-contained classroom, for example, recruit a catechetical team. Each team member studies one aspect of the curriculum in depth, becoming thoroughly comfortable with related lesson plans, then moves from class to class as needed. If they choose a different topic the following year, their knowledge level will increase again. On the other hand, if time pressures get in the way, they can continue teaching the same topic with a minimum of preparation time. These same folks might also enjoy leading an adult education session, talking to a small faith-sharing group, or being part of a day of reflection for parish leaders.

Each class might also have a non-teaching adviser who is with the students for every class. Those in the adviser role enjoy wonderful opportunities to learn more about their faith while overcoming their qualms about eventually taking on the role of teacher.

Meeting-weary volunteers will also appreciate a project approach. Instead of a monthly human concerns committee meeting, for example, the group could meet quarterly freeing more time to be part of a study group or to serve people in their area of interest. When they do meet, don't let them settle for a series of "then-we-did-this" reports. Make the meeting worth coming to by using the time to help volunteers practice people skills or learn better ways to listen, speak, or problem-solve. Set aside time for peer support and storytelling or engage the group in faith-sharing activities.

Job Descriptions

Written job and project descriptions benefit both your parish and parish-centered volunteers because they state how each job fits into the parish's overall mission and plans. Volunteers want to see their time and energy investment as service with a purpose. Writing a job description can also help the person seeking volunteers determine whether a particular job still adds value or is simply repeating timeworn activities that no longer serve the parish's mission effectively.

A useful job/project description:

- *clarifies expectations.* Well-thought-out job descriptions state what needs to be done by whom and by when. In preparing job descriptions, both staff and volunteers can achieve greater understanding of their respective roles in the parish.
- *helps match volunteers with work.* A well-written job description names the skills, time commitment, and personal characteristics needed to do specific work effectively. Volunteers who have or who have agreed to develop those qualifications are more likely to enjoy the job and do it well.
- *establishes a term of service.* Keeping the same person in the same job for two, ten, even twenty years underserves the parish and the person. A clearly stated term of service gives staff and volunteers the opportunity for a periodic review. Unhappy volunteers can bow out gracefully while volunteers who tend to stay and/or control an activity can be rerouted to another ministry without embarrassment.
- *can help potential volunteers be more discerning* about how a particular service is an appropriate response to their baptismal call and will help them grow spiritually.

If the thought of writing job descriptions seems a bit overwhelming, here are some tips.

- *Start slowly.* Focus on one area of volunteer ministry. Work with volunteers experienced in that area. Make the time you spend with them as important as getting the job done.
- *Keep it simple.* For each committee or group in that area, determine what jobs and how many people are needed to achieve the desired results. Then write job descriptions that answer questions potential volunteers will have. Use simple, clear language, limiting the text to a single page with lots of white space.

Quick tip: Adapt the sample job description on pages 73–74 for use in your parish.

The Volunteer's View

Preparing job/project descriptions makes it clear to prospective volunteers what work the parish needs them to do. Discovering what *volunteers* need, however, is what determines whether there will be an effective match. Yes, there will be times when we need to ask people to come forward just because the parish really needs help, but today's volunteers know that in a well-run parish, those times will be the exception. We already listed some of the things that attract people to parish volunteering in Chapter 4. Face-to-face conversations or "interviews" with prospects can help you discover which of those motivators are in place. People in many professions have also become familiar with personality testing and preference inventories and can tell you a great deal about what kind of volunteer work will be a good match for them.

Quick tip: Learn more about effective interviewing on pages 70, 74–75.

The concept of "career anchors" is one that may not have been considered in your parish. Through a longitudinal study and interviews, Edgar H. Schein, Ph.D., of the Alfred P. Sloan School of Management of the Massachusetts Institute of Technology identified eight types of career anchors. Knowing what these anchors are and how they attract people to certain kinds of work can add insight into what work is likely to be attractive to specific volunteers. The career anchors Schein identified are briefly summarized below. As you read through each description, list three or more types of work that volunteers who are motivated by that anchor might enjoy in your parish.

Technical/Functional Competence

Volunteers with a strong talent in a particular area are likely to enjoy using and developing skills in that area more than they will enjoy being responsible for overseeing or managing a project, program, or event. They prefer to work autonomously on projects that tests their abilities or skills (for example, fixing things, maintaining a parish garden, designing a newsletter) rather than being in charge of a group or handling administrative tasks. At Saints Alive, for example, Bill is skilled with budgeting and financial matters. Casey feels competent with graphic design. Neither is likely to volunteer to teach religious education until they feel a high level of competence with the subject matter. Casey, on the other hand, might be more than willing to edit the parish newsletter, especially if design decisions are not made by committee.

Parish volunteer work available for people with technical/functional competence:

_____

_____

General Managerial Competence

These volunteers like to be responsible for managing things in an organization. They are comfortable analyzing and solving problems as well as supervising or leading people at all levels. They will push for action-oriented decisions and make sure the next meeting date is set before leaving the current meeting. They want to work on projects that are important to the success of the organization and will happily chair committees, launch new projects. Janet, for example, is a volunteer who would be likely to chair the parish festival during the first year of her involvement. Rosa may also be attracted by this anchor, but her approach seems more low-key than Janet's.

Parish volunteer work available for people with general managerial competence:

_____

_____

Autonomy/Independence

Some volunteers like to do things their own way, at their own pace. They like to work independently on projects with clearly defined goals but with lots of flexibility as to how to go about meeting those goals. Though clearly anchored in functional competence both in his work as a mechanic and in his now thorough understanding of liturgical rites and rituals, Dan also seems willing to take an idea and run with it.

Volunteer work available for people with autonomy/independence competence:

_____

_____

Entrepreneurial Creativity

Entrepreneurial volunteers may see the parish as a place where they can express
their dreams of reshaping the world. They love to create and are likely to be
bored with repeating what has been done before. They would love to be involved
with parish planning, serve a term with the parish council, or design a brand-
new approach to stewardship.

Cheryl seems to be displaying some of the characteristics of a person who is
motivated by this anchor in her eagerness to explore volunteer/work match-
making.

Volunteer work available for people with entrepreneurial creativity competence:

_____

_____

Sense of Service, Dedication to a Cause

These volunteers are motivated to work toward certain values more than by any
specific talent or skill. They want to help people, improve society in general,
influence their own organization, and have an impact on social policies outside
of it. They are likely to begin their involvement through some type of human
concerns work. Like Harold, they may move quickly into leadership roles within
their specific area of interest.

Volunteer work available for people with service/dedication competence:

_____

_____

Pure Challenge

Some volunteers love to tackle unsolvable problems, overcome impossible obstacles to success. Though most people seek some level of challenge, this group is
motivated by challenge. The challenge may involve tackling a job that no one else
knows how to handle or dealing with a person others find difficult. Volunteers
motivated by pure challenge may be just whom you are looking for to facilitate a
collaborative venture with another parish or community group. Nate could have
settled for giving volunteer recruitment a boost but, almost immediately, he took
it several steps further, challenging himself and the group to a whole new way of
managing volunteer ministry.

Parish volunteer work available for people with pure challenge competency:

_____

_____

Lifestyle

Some volunteers make choices based on their current lifestyle. They want to help, but need to integrate volunteer opportunities comfortably into the rest of their lives. They may not be willing to give up time with their children to come to meetings, for example. Conversely, they may be looking for opportunities in which they can include their children. They may prefer volunteer opportunities that don't require coming to meetings at all. Homebound persons, for example, may find ways to volunteer using the Internet or telephone. Glenna and Rosa both need to think about family-based caregiving, yet each is an eager volunteer. The challenge with this group is to identify work that is meaningful for them. It also makes sense to discover other anchors that motivate them.

Parish volunteer work available for people with lifestyle competency:

_____

_____

Volunteer Ministry Planner 6: Be a Matchmaker

Choose one aspect of parish life that relies on volunteers. Invite one to three seasoned volunteers to prepare job descriptions for work that is currently being done in their area of volunteer ministry. Consider this as an opportunity to practice matching volunteers with work. Rather than ask people you know will say yes, take a few minutes to answer the following questions:

■ Who might be a match for this work? List three or more names.

_____

_____

_____

■ What skills will this work require? Some ideas are listed on the following page. Check the ones that apply to the process of writing job descriptions in the area of volunteer ministry you have chosen.

_____ experience with that area of parish life

_____ understanding of how the work in question moves the parish toward its mission

_____ ability to distinguish parts within the whole job

_____ ability to interview people who currently do that job

_____ ability to evaluate whether the job as it is best serves the arena of ministry

_____ other: _____

Hint: Plan to present this volunteer opportunity as a project. Work with the volunteers you recruit to establish clear goals, timelines, check-in points, and success factors. Be sure the volunteers know what resources and support are available. Plan how and when you will thank them for their efforts.

Writing Job/Project Descriptions

What will the job description look like? That's up to you. Choose a format that is easy to read [remember: we are moving into the era of aging eyes]. One page with lots of white space is best. Just be sure the prospective volunteer can find the answer to the following questions:

- What needs to be done by when?
- Why is this work important to the parish?
- What qualifications do I need?
- If I have some but not all of those qualifications, will I have the opportunity to learn and practice what I need to learn and practice?
- Where will I do the work?
- With whom?
- Where can I go with questions or problems?
- What is my budget? If I spend personal money, will I be reimbursed? How?
- What meetings/training sessions am I expected to attend?
- What records/reports am I expected to write?
- How long is my term of service?
- How will I benefit from doing this work?
- Other: _____

Once you have one or more completed job or project descriptions, brainstorm ways to put them to use.... Write a lively ad to fill one position.... Create a colorful poster with copies of several job descriptions from one area of parish-centered ministry.... Start a "ministry of the week" bulletin board by posting the job description with photos and testimony from volunteers who have served in that role.... Write a brief "feature story" for the parish newsletter or local paper about the volunteer who is currently doing similar work.... Fill a file box with all the job descriptions that have been completed to date and make it accessible to people who come to Mass.... Other: _____

The Next Step: Matching

In a community of disciples, volunteer managers do more than match prospects with work. Instead of just finding people to fill jobs, you find jobs to fill people. You help individuals identify what work they need to do next on this leg of their spiritual journeys. Interviewing is one tool that can help you do that.

> Hint: Become familiar with agencies and groups in your area that welcome volunteers. Understand their missions. Get to know their directors personally. Ask to be kept informed of new projects they undertake. Don't limit your thinking to human concerns projects. Many organizations need help with budgeting, legal issues, leadership development, planning, brochure design, board membership, and more—needs that someone in your parish might be delighted to meet if they knew such opportunities were available.

In parish-centered volunteer ministry, interviewing serves two purposes. We already explored the first—to find people who can and are willing to do specific parish work. The second is to find out what individuals need at this point in their spiritual journeys, then to walk with them while they discover opportunities to meet that need through volunteer service in or outside of the parish.

Though you may ask some of the same questions, interviewing potential volunteers isn't the same as interviewing a candidate for a staff job. It's more informal, like getting to know a new neighbor. Your goal is to get to know the potential volunteer personally, to initiate a relationship that enriches you both. Then, as needs arise, the names and faces of parishioners who could most effectively meet those needs tend to surface. When you contact them to ask for help, you can tell them specifically why they are being called instead of giving them the impression that you just pulled their name out of a hat or knew they couldn't say no. You have a genuine reason for asking them to get involved.

The bonus? When you initiate an ongoing interviewing process, you don't need to wait for an annual recruitment drive. You can interview potential volunteers anytime, formally or informally.

- *Start with current volunteers then expand your efforts.* Plan in advance to talk with one or two members before or after a scheduled committee meeting. Invite new parishioners for coffee and conversation four to six months after they register. When you are feeling adventurous, phone a parishioner who is not currently involved and ask if they would be willing to meet with you informally to learn more about parish-centered ministries.
- *Structure the interview with open-ended questions.* For example, what do you find attractive about our parish? What previous jobs (paid or volunteer) did you like the best? How would you describe the perfect volunteer job? Is there something you always wanted to know more about? Who was the best supervisor you ever had? Why? What other kinds of volunteer work are you already doing? What can you see yourself doing?
- *Use your sharpest listening skills.* Listen for hopes and dreams as well as skills and experience. Listen for a willingness to "job-share" or tackle one-time but intensive projects. Listen for need. Would the volunteer help more if child care were available? Would a single parent like to do something that would also include his children? Would the volunteer like to initiate something that is not currently being done in the parish? Can you discover what "anchors" are most likely to motivate this volunteer?
- *Don't make promises you can't keep.* Even if you have an urgent need to fill, don't lead potential volunteers on with promises of lots of help that isn't really available or by minimizing the time commitment. You may get them on board this time, but the next time you ask, they will head for the door.
- *Accept no for an answer.* Keep your relationship-building objective in mind. Stay in touch with potential volunteers without pressuring them to get involved. Call occasionally to ask for their reactions to a proposal. Personally invite them to hear speakers or participate in workshops they might find interesting, even if they are not already part of the team.

Micro-Perspective

- Practice interviewing the consistent volunteer you have already identified. Let him or her know that you want feedback. After the interview, you might want to ask some or all of the following questions: Am I modeling sincere hospitality? What image of "parish" am I presenting? Does it match with your expectations? How well did I listen? Is there anything you wish I hadn't done? What more would you have liked me to do? Be sure to thank the volunteer for his or her help.

- Now invite the person you identified who isn't volunteering to come in for an interview. Explain that your purpose is simply to practice and that you don't expect him or her to suddenly sign up for something. Go through the practice interview and ask for honest feedback using whatever questions above seem appropriate. Be sure to extend both a verbal and written thank you.

- Choose one of the recently completed job descriptions. Prospect for volunteers who might be interested in filling that job. Follow-up on the responses and set up interviews. Find one or more matches. If others respond that don't seem to be good matches, work the process in reverse. Invite them for an interview and help them discover an opportunity that is right for them.

"This sounds like an awful lot of work," Bill said. "Why don't we just go back to the old time/talent form? Revise it if you want but keep it efficient."

"Marge is not going to be happy about this either," Nate said. "It's way too much information to key into a computer."

"This isn't about building a database," Rosa said. "It's about building relationships. Like it or not, relationships take work."

"We have choices," said Dan. "If we really want to involve more parishioners in volunteering, we have to improve what they experience here. If we want efficiency, that's fine. But then we need to stop complaining about the results."

"I'm for efficiency," Bill said.

"I think I am too though I have to admit that being part of this team has been a lot more satisfying than the stuff you, I mean the parish, used to ask me to do," said Glenna. She stooped to grab Joshua Alexander who had found a stack of old bulletins and was laying them end to end across the floor.

"I'm torn," said Janet, bending down to help Glenna pick up the paper trail. "I'm all for efficiency, but after meeting with you all, I've learned some things I didn't know before. And I came in here thinking I knew just about everything about this parish."

Rosa picked up one of the bulletins after Josh put it back on the floor. The readings for the following Sunday were printed inside.

"Listen to this," she said.

> On this mountain the Lord of hosts
> will provide for all peoples
> a feast of rich food and choice wines,
> juicy, rich food and pure, choice wines.
> On this mountain he will destroy
> the veil that veils all peoples,
> The web that is woven over all nations;
> he will destroy death forever.
> The Lord God will wipe away the tears from all faces;
> The reproach of his people he will remove
> from the whole earth; for the Lord has spoken.
> On that day it will be said:
> "Behold our God to whom we looked to save us!
> This is the Lord for whom we looked;
> let us rejoice and be glad that he has saved us!"
> For the hand of the Lord will rest on this mountain...
>
> (ISAIAH 25:6–10)

"Wow," said Glenna. "Remember when the volunteer center director was here? She told us that Catholics volunteer in the community more than any other religious-affiliated group. If that's true, and if Isaiah knew what he was talking about, there must be more than enough volunteers to go around. Instead of always focusing on scarcity, maybe we should try focusing on abundance."

"I agree," Rosa said. "It's a better match for this organization. I also think it's about time we started trusting diversity."

"You mean we should try recruiting more people of color and from different ethnic groups?" Adele asked.

"Of course we should be doing that," said Rosa. "But when it comes to volunteering, I think diversity takes on an even broader meaning. Just as we talked about structuring volunteer positions in different ways, we want to honor diversity of interests, diversity of gifts, diversity of "anchors," and so on. Matching is about getting in touch with all the diversity in the parish and bringing out the best in it."

Practical Matters 6

Sample Job Description

Please adapt this format to suit the needs of people in your parish.

Job/Project name: _____

Summary of work:

_____

When: _____

Where: _____

By whom? _____

With whom? _____

Accountable to: _____

The work is important to the parish because:

_____

_____

_____

What qualifications will make the work easier?

_____

_____

_____

What learning opportunities go along with taking this position?

_____

_____

_____

What training is required?

_____

_____

_____

What resources are available to support this work? (for example, financial, other volunteers, staff involvement, and so on)

_____

_____

_____

Primary contact for answers to questions, help with solving problems, and so on:

_____

_____

_____

Personal expenditures up to _____ will be reimbursed by _____ .

Advance approval required for additional expenditures.

- Required meetings: _____
- Required written reports: _____
- Term of service: _____

[Add any other information that volunteers will need to know to complete this work effectively.]

Interview Notes

Rather than designing an official form for your interview process, take informal notes. Aim for a conversational tone during the interview. Do write down a name, home and e-mail addresses, phone and fax numbers. Beyond that information, just note key ideas you want to remember. Invite the person with whom you are meeting to jot down notes as well. This is not a one-up/one-down hiring process, just two people exploring possibilities that will serve them both well.

Some notes you might want to make include what the person likes best about your parish, what programs and activities they think are really being done well, paid and volunteer jobs they have especially enjoyed in their lives, what kinds of people with whom they are most comfortable and most uncomfortable working. Setting up either/or scenarios can uncover more information without prying. Start out a series of choices with an opener that goes something like this:

- "If you had to choose one or the other, would you rather..."

  - work with children or with older persons?
  - work here at the parish or out in the community?
  - work here or at home?
  - raise money or plan how to spend it?
  - welcome new parishioners or visit the sick?

Reflecting on Age Diversity

Diversity is an important issue. As Rosa pointed out, by now every parish should be honoring racial, ethnic, and cultural diversity. When it comes to parish volunteering, however, it is diversity of gifts, interests, and place in one's spiritual journey that matters most. Create many opportunities for people in your parish to explore and experience every kind of diversity. The workshop planned below focuses on one aspect of diversity that impacts every parish volunteer—generational diversity. Feel free to use the plan as is, or adapt it to meet your needs.

God's Mix *Time: 2 hrs.*

Who should attend: committee chairs, staff, group officers, anyone interested in learning more about making the most of intergenerational differences in parish life; for best results, aim to have more than one representative from each intergenerational category.

I. Opening Activity: Hum a Few Bars...

Draw a parish time line from founding to present. Invite the group to identify milestones with dates (approximate will do) over the parish's current life span. Encourage people who were parishioners at the time to talk about what they most remember about that event. Listen to their stories. Under each parish milestone, ask participants to name key community, nation, world events that may have been happening at the same time. Inventions? Sports heroes? Communication media? Clothing styles? Ask people to recall a song popular at that time. Hum a few bars or sing out a whole refrain.

II. Name Some Apparent Differences Between Age Groups

Pass out copies of pages 78–79 that list characteristics of four distinct age groups. Ask members of that age group what they think of the characteristics mentioned.

Break

III. Quiz: How Do We Shape Up Diversity-Wise?

[Ask people to complete this survey individually, then meet in small groups to discuss their answers. After five to ten minutes, discuss answers with the large group.]

- Our committees, groups, and leaders are made up of a mix of ages, sexes, and ethnicity.

  False   Somewhat false   Somewhat true   True

- When we form a committee or group, we consciously include people of different ages, backgrounds, experiences, viewpoints.

  Never   Rarely   Occasionally   Usually   Always

- We welcome and take time to talk about differing viewpoints.

  Never   Rarely   Occasionally   Usually   Always

- We plan volunteer work around individual preferences.

  Never   Rarely   Occasionally   Usually   Always

- If truth be told, there is a lot of "behind the back" talking about committee members and/or parish leaders.

  Never   Rarely   Occasionally   Usually   Always

- Our work atmosphere is relaxed, even playful.

  Never   Rarely   Occasionally   Usually   Always

- Volunteers communicate in a straightforward manner.

  Never   Rarely   Occasionally   Usually   Always

- Parish leaders communicate in a straightforward manner.

  Never   Rarely   Occasionally   Usually   Always

- We treat every parishioner as if he/she has great things to offer.

  Never   Rarely   Occasionally   Usually   Always

IV. Working With Age Diversity

Spend ten minutes in small groups discussing how to address the scenario below. Ask each small group to report their response to the large group.

- Scenario

Your parish recently set "increasing diverse participation in all parish activities" as its primary goal for the year. You have agreed to chair the committee that plans and prepares Sunday morning coffees in the church hall. Current committee members say they need more help. Prospective volunteers say they have offered to help but were never called or felt unwelcome when they tried to get involved. How will you proceed?

V. How Is Your Current Approach to Age Diversity Affecting What Volunteers Experience in Your Parish?

- What seems to be working well relative to age diversity?
- What needs improvement?

VI. What's Your Vision for Age Diversity?

VII. What Might Be a Next Step?

Differences Between Age Groups

People Born Before/During World War II:

First to experience: Superman, Winston Churchill, Babe Ruth, Mickey Mouse, Dagwood, Lone Ranger, Lindbergh, D-Day, Roosevelt, Korean War, Joe McCarthy, radio

Said to be: conservative, dedicated, hard-working, conforming, disciplined, detail-oriented, reluctant to buck the system

Understand: law/order, delayed reward, adherence to rules, honor, respect, loyalty

Want to know: that their experience is respected

Tend to be: organizationally hierarchical with one person in charge

Post-World War II to Kent State:

First to experience: Polio shots, Rosa Parks, Civil Rights, JFK, Peace Corps, MLK, moon landing, Woodstock, Ed Sullivan, TV, slinkies, Vietnam, credit cards, imported automobiles

Said to be: growth & expansion oriented, children in the spotlight, optimistic, cool, judgmental

Understand: teamwork, personal growth as a value, redefined male/female roles, rewritten rules

Tend to be: challenging authority, expecting personal gratification, involved, driven, willing to go the extra mile, good at relationships, uncomfortable with conflict/feedback

Want to know: their work is valued, unique, and important

Born 1960–80:

First to experience: women's liberation, Arab terrorists, Watergate, PCs, Fall of Berlin Wall, Exxon Valdes oil spill, Brady Bunch, Simpsons, single-parent homes, cellular phones, fast food, answering machines, post-college trips to Europe, *Ferris Bueller's Day Off,* student loans

Said to be: global thinkers, informal, self-reliant, pragmatic, fun-loving

Understand: casual approaches to authority, technology, Internet, and e-mail

Tend to be: seeking balance, technologically savvy, not especially interested in politics, hard-working, many are struggling to make ends meet while others have high incomes at an early age

Want to know: that they are not being taken advantage of

Born 1980–2000:

First to experience: busy activity-filled childhoods, stress, Clinton/Lewinsky, Columbine High School, Barney, Beanie Babies, He-Man, Oprah, Spice Girls, Mark McGwire, Bill Gates, personal pagers

Said to be (so far): optimistic, confident, sociable, smart, street smart, diversity savvy, collective-oriented

Understand: achievement, multi-tasking

Tend to be: inexperienced, tenacious, in need of supervision and structure

Want to know: how to accomplish big things; experts believe this group will strive to make heroes of themselves

[Adapted from Ron Zemke with Claire Raines and Bob Filipczak (2000), *Generations at Work: Managing the Clash of Veterans, Boomers, Xers, and Nexters in Your Workplace*. New York: Amacom American Management Association.]

CHAPTER SEVEN

Combustion

W e have problems," said Dan. "Problems we should deal with right away."
The volunteer ministry planning group was meeting in Rosa's dining room as they had several times during the past year. Now homebound, Abuela still sat nearby. Joshua Alexander's interruptions wouldn't be a problem, at least for this evening. Rosa's son was on a break from his classes at the community college and Rosa had recruited him to take Joshua to the park.

Since the group met often at Rosa's now, her neighbor Roberto and others from Crosstown parish joined the discussions.

"What problems, Dan? More rumors?" Roberto asked.

Throughout the past few months, rumors had circulated about closing Crosstown parish and merging it with Saints Alive. Everyone looked at Nate, then at Bill, for an update but both men were silent.

"I for one am opposed to the idea," said Janet. "That many new people would be a real drain on our resources. Besides, we're too different."

"Rumors aren't our problem, at least not yet," Dan said. "Cheryl, Rosa, Casey, and I just spent the last three months meeting with committees at both parishes to get input on the next phase of planning for volunteer ministry. Some people complained that the volunteers they recruit don't stay."

"We should do a survey," Janet said, "to find out why the people who left didn't come back."

"That could be helpful," Rosa said, "but it might make more sense to talk with the volunteers who *do* come back and find out what keeps them motivated."

Janet glared at Rosa. "That approach won't tell us anything we don't already know."

"I'm just going by what one of our parishioners said to me when I invited her to join us," Rosa said. "She said, 'Of course I'll come. I want what you have.'"

"Well, what *do* we have?" Deacon Nate asked. "We've been working together a good long time now. Why do you all keep coming back?"

"Our work means something to the parish," said Dan. "What we are doing here makes a difference—at least in the liturgy committee."

"I come because I feel good about what we are accomplishing," Casey said. "We haven't pressured ourselves to change things overnight or to do things perfectly. But things are changing just the same."

"I agree," said Rosa. "I've been a parish volunteer since my son started school, almost twenty years now. But this is the first time I have really felt supported. I don't feel taken for granted or trapped into doing something that I can't get out of."

"I like that this group only meets when it needs to," Bill said. "That makes it easier for me. You know I like to keep abreast of what's happening in the parish."

"I come for the study," said Cheryl. "I would never read Scripture or talk about these ideas like discipleship on my own. At first, the study part seemed like a waste of meeting time. Now I can see how our discussions help us make better plans."

"We can skip you, Nate," Dan said. "You have to be here."

"Are you kidding? All Father Ralph expected me to do was bump up recruitment," Nate said. "We accomplished that last year. I come because I think we are on to something more here. I can't begin to tell you how much I value what all of you bring to the table!"

"Thank you," said Adele. "I *do* feel appreciated and I also feel as if I belong here. The more we tell our stories, the more comfortable I get, like it's OK for me to be my true self here."

"That's sounding a little too touchy-feely for me," Bill said. "I don't need to reveal my true self to run a pledge campaign."

"Well, I'm willing to reveal some of my true self right now," said Harold. "Before I got involved with the global justice discussion groups, I only kept coming so I could get closer to Adele. It worked! In fact, we have an announcement to make. We're engaged!"

Far too often, people who manage parish-centered volunteers worry more about recruiting new people than they do about retaining the volunteers they already have. The real work of management, however, involves drawing the most from all of an organization's resources in order to effectively and efficiently fulfill its mission. Retaining people is an important responsibility of management.

In any organization, a manager's job is likely to be complex and ongoing. Each aspect of the work requires planning, organizing, leading others in implementation, and monitoring progress. In a parish, however, carrying out those four functions are only part of the picture because we acknowledge the Holy Spirit as the ultimate volunteer ministry manager. That means that while doing all we can to plan, organize, lead, and monitor effectively, volunteer ministry managers are also entrusted with sustaining an environment where the Holy Spirit can work. We can find some clues about effective ways to go about that by looking at Scripture and by listening to what people guided by that Spirit have to say.

Lessons From Scripture

A quick read of the gospels can leave us with the impression that once Jesus' disciples answered his call, they felt more or less compelled to tag along in the follower mode. As the story of the gospels unfolds, we discover that Jesus didn't plan to use the tag-along, follower mode of "managing" his disciples. He intended to turn his entire mission over to those disciples. Rather than "forming" them as receivers and disseminators of sacred information, he exposed them to the kinds of things they would need to do as proclaimers of good news. Though he frequently put wisdom into words for them, his primary teaching tool was modeling the behaviors he wanted them to live out and allowing them to witness the results. As a result, their primary learning tool was hands-on experience with miracles.

Consider Matthew 4:23–25:

Jesus toured all of Galilee. He taught in their synagogues, proclaimed the good news of the kingdom, and cured the people of every disease and illness. As a consequence, his reputation traveled the length of Syria. They carried to him all those afflicted with various diseases and racked with pain: the possessed, the lunatics, the paralyzed. He cured them all. The great crowds that followed him came from Galilee, the Ten Cities, Jerusalem and Judea, and from across the Jordan.

Think about what those early days must have been like for the newly called disciples. They learned, heard good news, saw important work—healing work—being accomplished, seemingly without regard for status or qualifications, with astonishing results. People wanted what Jesus had. The *disciples* wanted what Jesus had. They recognized that staying around offered them the best chance of getting it.

Eleven Ways to Generate Retention

Each of the twelve management factors described below can strengthen parish-centered volunteer ministry. Incorporating even one of them into your plans will enrich what people who volunteer experience in your parish and is likely to motivate them to keep coming back.

1. Offer Meaningful Work

Meaningful work must be, first of all, of real value to the organization. When we can sincerely explain how the work we ask volunteers to do truly matches the parish's mission, volunteers are likely to see even envelope stuffing as meaningful to the parish. On the other hand, Post-Vatican II Catholics know the core practices of the parish life and are considerably less likely to cheerfully engage in work that only gives lip service to mission. Well-written job/project descriptions go a long way toward ensuring that the work we ask volunteers to do is truly meaningful to the parish.

Volunteers will also want work that is meaningful to them personally. Respecting where people are on their spiritual journeys and what "anchors" people to work goes a long way toward ensuring that what we ask volunteers to do is meaningful to them as individuals. Today's volunteers look for evidence that the proposed work is truly meaningful to the parish. What will they look for?

- *Work that helps meet one or more specific short-term or long-term goals.* Instead of saying, "The director of religious education needs these envelopes stuffed," your envelope stuffing crew wants to hear you say, "Our goal is to make sure that every parent of a teenager in this parish has accurate information about preparing for the sacrament of Confirmation."
- *Work that is important enough to be supported by budget, training, and ongoing interaction with the pastoral and/or direction-setting leaders of the parish.* Instead of saying, "Tell your friends we need more people to help out with the meal program," members of your human concerns committee want to hear you say, "The parish council is committed to increasing outreach to the poor. They've set aside funds for speakers, field trips, and other awareness-raising activities, and want us to design a plan that will involve many more people in activities like the meal program."
- *Work for which they will be held accountable for results.* Instead of saying, "We need everyone to speak clearly and with enthusiasm," your lectors want to hear you say, "When you speak clearly and with enthusiasm, you can sense the energy and involvement of the people who are listening to the readings.

That's what we are aiming for and that is what we are counting on you to do."

- *Work that offers appropriate recognition for a job well done.* It isn't unusual to see articles in a parish bulletin announcing the success of a fundraiser or building program and specifically praising a handful of individuals who helped create that success. Less common are articles acknowledging the work of specific individuals for attending weekly choir rehearsals, making sandwiches for the homeless, or daily phoning a homebound parishioner.

When your parish isn't willing or able to make those kinds of commitments in-house, volunteers will look to other organizations and groups who can.

2. Schedule Orientations to Set the Tone

Effective orientations draw new volunteers even more fully into parish-centered ministry. At some parishes, volunteer managers plan a half- or full-day retreat for all new volunteers. Others schedule a two- to three-hour evening session. Some schedule more than one session, giving volunteers the opportunity to spend several months to a year in study, networking, spiritual development, service exploration, and field trips. Still others plan an annual retreat or day of reflection for all parish volunteers, inviting new people to come early for a session geared specifically to their needs.

Design your orientations to meet the following goals:

- deeper understanding of how the work relates to the parish's mission
- awareness of or development of short-term objectives
- firm basis for effective communication
- sincere sense of belonging
- clarity about what the parish expects from volunteers
- clarity about what volunteers can expect from the parish

3. Schedule Worthwhile Training as Needed

Training needs will vary from ministry to ministry, but every volunteer will need at least one job-specific training session that fleshes out the job/project description and answers any questions they may have about what resources are available to them and where they can go for help. In some cases, training can be combined with orientation, but be sure your plan doesn't substitute one for the other.

4. Respect Everyone As They Are

The issue of respect covers everything from appropriate matching to valuing volunteers' time to helping them find resources to working with them to solve a problem to walking with them through a difficult learning experience to adapting plans to meet their scheduling needs. Effective managers don't spend their energy trying to "form" volunteers to fit the culture of the organization. They respect volunteers as they are and invest their own energies in managing (planning, organizing, leading others in implementation of, and monitoring the progress of) the work.

5. Model Community

"Because it is done in the company of others, work remains one of the more important ways we have of finding ourselves," wrote Dick Westley, author of *Good Things Happen: Experiencing Community in Small Groups.* People bond when they complete work together and experience a common feeling of satisfaction. That bonding, however, is only a "foretaste of a more profound and deeper unity stemming from a bonding of selves, the uniting of spirits which is the hallmark of community in its fullest form. To become community, the bonding and togetherness of the workplace must touch and call forth our deepest truest selves."

The longing for real community is a key reason why people seek out parish-centered volunteering. Using the management approach described in this resource contributes to that sense of community. It expects volunteer work to evolve from shared vision and purpose rather than from how things have been done in the past. It makes the most of commonly understood images of the parish striving to be what it says it is. It plans for constant and challenging learning experiences through which individuals can explore spirituality in the context of meaningful work.

In the final three sections of this resource, we will discuss how the approach honors the seasons of the human life span, ensuring that God's people will ever be moving in and out of the roles of servant and served. That last expectation applies equally to the manager and the managed, calling both to be their true selves in all situations.

Westley stressed that community is pure gift. There are no how-tos for creating it and no certainty that it will be a natural by-product of working together. You can't mandate or force community; you can't design it or market it into being. When people who manage volunteers let go of their desire to control, then model the behaviors Jesus wanted us to live out, they sustain an environment where community can happen.

6. Share Faith

In 1974, the process through which adults come into the Church shifted from an emphasis on instruction to an emphasis on learning from the faith stories of others. In the sharing, everyone's faith was strengthened. That same experience can happen in volunteer settings. Ironically, in a story-sharing environment, it also becomes easier to manage the work that needs to be done.

Effective managers encourage volunteers to incorporate faith-based practices like Scripture reading, faith-sharing, silence, prayer, discernment, and song into their gatherings when it seems appropriate to do so. Incorporating any one of these practices is appropriate *when the choice will enrich the work,* not just for the sake of artificially injecting spiritual moments into a business meeting. Struggling with a decision might signal a need to incorporate prayer and discernment, for example. Storytelling or faith-sharing might be appropriate when trying to generate new ideas or alternatives. A lively song might jump-start a meeting; listening to quiet music might soothe fragile nerves after a heated debate.

How do we motivate volunteers to keep coming back? Fill their hunger for a real faith community. Help them find it among fellow volunteers. Make them want what you have.

7. Ensure Continuous Learning Opportunities

Beyond job-specific training, open doors to a variety of learning opportunities. Keep volunteers informed about relevant workshops and conferences offered through the diocese, other parishes, community colleges, universities, and other groups. Encourage them to share what they learned with parish-centered volunteers.

8. Expect Needs

Revisit the matching process to help volunteers discover how work they do through the parish can help them meet their own needs. When needs are all-consuming, cheerfully offer to find other volunteers who can get the work done while the current volunteer gets his or her needs met. If the parish can help, do so. In any case, stay in touch with your first volunteer. Let the person know he or she is valued even when they aren't available to help.

9. Expect Charisms

One role of the community is to help people discover their charisms, qualities that have been described as those special gifts of the Holy Spirit given as needed for the common good.

"Trying to define them is like trying to bottle wind or package fire since they take as many forms as there are individuals receiving them," wrote John C. Haughey, S.J. "One conclusion I have reached after studying much about the subject is that they enable many people to do ordinary things extraordinarily well. Occasionally, charisms enable a few people to do extraordinary things. If we think of them only in this latter sense, that is, something out of the ordinary, we easily miss their presence among us or in us."[1]

As someone who manages parish-centered volunteers, you are in a key position to help people become more comfortable with the presence of charisms in the community. According to Doris Donnely, that calls for being open to at least three surprises.

- Charisms emerge among people in the world as well as among people within ecclesial institutions.
- Charisms may be found wherever there are human needs.
- Charisms are unique gifts given for the common good.[2]

Some are wary of exposing the community to a full awareness of its potential for charism. Others eagerly embrace the concept. Whatever your position, it makes sense to learn as much as you can about charisms, remain open to the possibility, and leave the rest to the Holy Spirit.

10. Create Spirit Space for Volunteers

Volunteers may not say so, but having a space of their own can make their experience more satisfying. Equally important, having some sort of "headquarters" could help you manage more effectively. Look around the parish for a space, large or small, that could be set aside for the exclusive use of parish-centered volunteers.

Whether it's a room, a closet, or a corner in a larger room, aim to make it welcoming with colorful posters or bulletin boards that announce meetings and trainings. Post photos, success stories, interesting articles, book reviews, tips for effectiveness, motivational quotes. Offer sticky-notes for messages or feedback on a topic. Tuck a stash of juice boxes or granola bars in a drawer. Make it fun. Be on the lookout for jokes, cartoons, quick quizzes, and games volunteers might enjoy.

1. Donnely, Doris, ed. *Retrieving Charisms for the Twenty-first Century.* Collegeville, MN: Liturgical Press, 1999.
2. *Ibid.*

11. Say "Thank You" Frequently, Specifically, and Personally

Volunteers may tell you they don't need to be thanked, don't want recognition. Don't believe them. They may not want to be made the center of attention at some recognition event, but everyone likes to be appreciated.

Though we don't read of Jesus saying "thank you" to his disciples in so many words, we still talk about when he surprised them with a delightful seaside brunch, how he publicly praised a widow's paltry contribution, the time he trusted a woman with a questionable past to carry his message.

Effective volunteer managers say thank you and say it often. They also find other ways to affirm what volunteers bring to parish life. They say "thank you" by trusting volunteers with important work, making it possible for them to grow in skills and experience, striving to develop satisfying relationships with them, no matter how minimal their contribution. They thank people who volunteer outside of the parish, publicly acknowledging how their service enriches the mission of the church. Consider how your parish might support these larger efforts. Organize a small faith-sharing group for people who volunteer in the community. Pray for community volunteers during the Sunday liturgy. Post volunteer opportunities beyond parish boundaries as well as those available in your parish.

Volunteer Ministry Planner 7: Generate Retention Day by Day

Review your vision and purpose statements for parish-centered volunteer ministry last revised on page 20. How could practicing each of the retention-generators described below move volunteers in your parish closer to that vision? Record your answers in your planning notebook.

RETENTION GENERATORS

Offering meaningful work
Scheduling inspiring orientations
Scheduling worthwhile training
Respecting everyone as they are
Modeling community
Sharing faith

Ensuring continuous learning
  opportunities
Expecting needs
Expecting charisms
Creating Spirit-space for volunteers
Saying thank you regularly

Micro-Perspective

Plan to evaluate your own growth as a manager of parish-centered volunteers at least twice each year. What are your strongest management skills? Where could you use improvement? On the list below, check the ones that you do well and those that need improvement.

MANAGEMENT SKILL	OK	NEEDS IMPROVEMENT
I see volunteers as disciples on a spiritual journey.	❏	❏
I practice ongoing recruitment.	❏	❏
I encourage every volunteer to stretch.	❏	❏
I continually operate in a learning mode.	❏	❏
I focus on volunteers' strengths instead of weaknesses.	❏	❏
I set direction, then trust volunteers to meet the goal.	❏	❏
I serve as a worthwhile resource to volunteers.	❏	❏
I offer volunteers meaningful work.	❏	❏
I schedule interesting orientations.	❏	❏
I schedule interesting training sessions.	❏	❏
I consistently model "community."	❏	❏
I do all I can to help meet volunteers' needs.	❏	❏
I've done all I can to create "Spirit-space" for volunteers.	❏	❏
I help volunteers find hidden talents and expect charisms.	❏	❏
I say thank you often.	❏	❏

Which area of improvement would most enrich what you experience as a manager of volunteers?

How would improving in this area benefit you?

Picture a reluctant volunteer that you wish to retain. Improving which area of volunteer management would most benefit that volunteer? How?

If you chose to improve one of the two skills you identified above, how would that help you generate retention?

If you decided to improve in that area, what would be the next step? Check any that apply.

_____ seek advice in management books
_____ enroll in a class or workshop on the topic
_____ ask for one-on-one help
_____ find a mentor
_____ other: _____

Are you willing to take that step? ___ Yes ___ No
When?

Gratitude-Based Motivators

Check each of the following "thank you's" that are used in your parish volunteer program.

_____ Say "thank you" by phone or in person
_____ Write thank-you notes
_____ Offer on-site treats
_____ Create original, inexpensive gifts (bookmarks, candy)
_____ Offer opportunities to network
_____ Offer opportunities to represent the parish elsewhere
_____ Involve volunteers in important decisions
_____ Remember birthdays and other special occasions
_____ Assign authority
_____ Plan parties, celebrations
_____ Post photos of volunteers on the job
_____ Pick up the tab for advanced workshops/trainings
_____ Create a bulletin board that gives credit for work
_____ Total hours contributed by all volunteers
_____ Invite families to celebrate successes
_____ Ask your pastor to write a letter of thanks
_____ Share thank-you notes from people who have been helped through volunteer efforts
_____ Plan a field trip
_____ Send articles about volunteers to newspapers
_____ Follow up on their ideas
_____ Never send them on guilt-trips

List the names of three parish-centered volunteers on the following page. Choose one expression of gratitude from the list above that would be meaningful to that volunteer. Pick a time and place to express your gratitude to him or her in that way.

NAMES	EXPRESSION OF GRATITUDE	WHEN?

∿

"Glenna, you never told us why you keep coming to these meetings," Adele said. "It can't be easy for you having to always bring Josh along."

Glenna didn't answer right away. Across the table, Janet and Rosa had reopened the discussion about whom to survey. Cheryl, Casey, and Dan were comparing notes on the committees they had visited.

"Is everything OK, Glenna?" Adele asked.

"No!" Glenna burst into tears. "Everything is not all right! My husband packed his bag three weeks ago. I don't think he is coming back."

She put her face in her hands. "I don't know if I'll be able to keep coming here. I need a job. I need to go back to school. But I need this group too, now more than ever."

Abuela rose slowly and left the room. Moments later the first notes from Liszt's *Un Sospiro* rolled from the upright. Glenna was crying softly, and Adele had put her arm around Glenna's shoulder.

Practical Matters 7

Jump-Start Meetings!

Every committee meeting doesn't need to be like the last. When volunteers can walk out the door saying, "That was a good meeting!" you can be sure they will be back for more. What makes a "good" meeting? Most volunteers describe a good meeting as one during which people enjoyed creative thinking, a relaxed atmosphere, and a sense of satisfaction about what was accomplished. Four simple activities can jump-start those kinds of meetings.

- *Joke around.* It's OK to have fun during a meeting even when the issues you are dealing with are serious. Let good humor flow. Sometimes the best ideas come from combining elements of two or more suggestions that sounded downright silly at first.
- *Undo your assumptions.* Assume the committee is starting from scratch and has no history to live up to. What would you do? Approach every agenda

item in a seeking mode. Instead of settling for the first answer offered, keep asking "what if…?" or "why not…?"

- *Move.* Meet in a different location or at a different time of day. Walk around the parish grounds. Try to imagine what people might need from your committee in five years. What can you do now to help meet those needs? At least change chairs (both kinds)! Invite a committee member or someone who is not part of your committee to facilitate a brainstorming session. As for the other kind of chair…have you noticed that people tend to sit in the same places meeting after meeting? Change places. You might be surprised at how a different "view" can give you a different perspective.
- *Put it on the wall.* Don't settle for linear thinking. Get a poster board or use the chalkboard and literally draw out your ideas. Try grouping different ideas with lines and circles. Try drawing a path from "here" to "there." Use sticky-notes to move ideas around. See what evolves.

Welcome every idea but, whatever you do, don't assume that the person offering a new idea will be the one to implement it. Nothing stalls input faster than thinking that any idea you suggest will automatically fall back in your lap.

Jump-start your next meeting by preparing effective meeting notes. Valuable meeting notes include the following items:

- Date the last meeting was held
- Who was present
- Discussion items with key points to remember italicized
- Action items with key decisions in bold type. Each action item should include a summary of objectives, strategies, agreed upon measures of success, and a list of who will do what by when.
- Brief report summaries
- Next meeting date
- Name of person who prepared the meeting notes

What Would You Do?

If you are serious about retaining volunteers, it makes sense to think ahead about situations that might develop. Some volunteers leave after experiencing serious conflict (see Chapter 8). Most volunteers who leave, however, just fade out of the picture. A little advance planning might just create a different result. Try your hand at the following cases.

Case #1

Chuck was a member of the parish finance committee for four years. He worked hard to promote the annual fund drive, put in long hours organizing a special debt reduction effort, enthusiastically presented new ideas, and supported the suggestions of other committee members. Then suddenly Chuck quit.

Some speculated that there were problems at home. Others thought he was disappointed by the results of a recent parish council decision. Still others thought he was frustrated by the new business manager's apparent misunderstanding of the role of the finance committee.

What was Chuck's reason for walking away from his volunteer role? No one ever asked. At year-end, a survey was sent to all parish volunteers. It included an open-ended question: how could we improve what you experienced as a volunteer here?

"Call me," Chuck wrote. But no one ever did.

If you were the person managing volunteers at Chuck's parish, what would you do next?

❑ Nothing. It's too late to deal with this situation effectively.
❑ Send Chuck another copy of the survey and hope he sends it back.
❑ Ask the business manager if he knows anything about why Chuck left.
❑ Call Chuck today and see if you can talk him into coming back.
❑ Call Chuck and apologize for letting so much time go by without contact.
❑ Ask Chuck if he'd be willing to meet with you to talk over the situation.

Prepared surveys can give us clues about things we need to do to improve what volunteers experience, but they can't tell the whole story. And when a volunteer requests follow-up that never happens, it only makes a bad situation worse.

If you really want to know what volunteers are experiencing, get information from people. Find out if volunteers feel they are valued and being treated with respect, doing meaningful work, receiving the training and tools they need to do a good job, growing spiritually through their volunteer efforts. Ask them what they want, then be prepared to follow through or at the very least explain why you can't.

All Chuck wanted was a phone call. Would a call have made a difference? There are no guarantees, but consider the possibilities.

- *Problems at home.* A caller could have offered a listening ear, suggested a helpful resource, or promised to pray for him. Even if Chuck did not choose to disclose personal information, knowing that others cared and were available to listen could make a real difference in how Chuck feels about his parish.

- *Dissatisfied with a parish council decision.* A caller might have clarified misinformation or linked Chuck with a council member who could work through the issue with Chuck.
- *Frustrated over the business manager's interpretation.* A caller might have thanked Chuck for naming the issue and encouraged the committee chair to lead the entire group, including the business manager, in reviewing their understanding of the committee's role together.

A call might have accomplished two things: provided information about what wasn't working well and let Chuck know he was valued even when he wasn't volunteering. For a ministry dedicated to serving others, it is just common sense— if you want to know what someone needs, ask.

Case #2

Chairperson Jerry hoped to recruit three new members for the finance committee but, by October, he only had one new member. "Oh well, one is better than none," he said, and confidently plunged into the business at hand.

By February, just as major deadlines for finance committee projects were looming, one of the finance committee's most experienced members was transferred. Another simply stopped coming to meetings. Committee members completed all of their projects but turned several in late and were less than satisfied with the results. At year-end, only Jerry and one person agreed to serve with the finance committee the following year.

If you were managing volunteers at Jerry's parish, how would you have handled things?

❑   I would have done just what Jerry did.
❑   I would have reduced the number of projects the finance committee would handle.
❑   I would have immediately pushed deadlines forward wherever possible.
❑   I would have continued to recruit until we reached our goal of three new members.
❑   All of the above.

Jerry really set his committee up for disappointment when he stopped recruiting the volunteers they needed. Like dropping that last five pounds on a diet, finding those last few volunteers for a committee seems to be the most difficult recruitment task. It's tempting to just be grateful for the volunteers you have and stop trying. While that approach may work in the short run, it doesn't serve your parish over the long term. Here's why:

- *You may be breaking promises.* Many a volunteer has been told, "don't worry, you will have plenty of help," only to find themselves carrying the bulk of the burden alone. Though they may not complain, such volunteers are unlikely to say yes again. They may also talk about their negative experience with prospective volunteers who, in turn, decide not to say yes.
- *You may be shortchanging your committee.* New volunteers come with insights and ideas, and raise old but challenging questions that the committee somehow always manages to avoid answering. Bringing in new members usually turns out to be a learning experience for everyone.
- *You may be supporting the "same old people" syndrome.* Parishioners often complain that the same people do everything. The unspoken belief is that newcomers aren't welcome on existing committees. When you stop trying to recruit volunteers, that message is reinforced.
- *You may be inadvertently helping people to miss the point of volunteer ministry.* Most committees stress that volunteers will be drawn more fully into parish life by taking on important tasks and responsibilities. More important, however, is their call to discipleship, the experience of ongoing learning about how God works in the world. Overburdened volunteers may feel more like martyrs than disciples. If the committee has more work than it can handle easily, recruiting those last few volunteers is essential.

In addition to continuing his recruitment efforts, Jerry may also have decided to eliminate all but the most essential work that year and move deadlines as far forward as possible.

Case #3

Carlos had been asking Peggy for weeks to chair the religious education committee. A long-time member, Peggy knew a lot about religious ed programs offered, had a reputation for being a cracker-jack organizer, and knew how to get a job done.

The last time Peggy chaired a committee, however, she had been miserable. She hadn't found enough volunteers. Those she did recruit argued among themselves, didn't do what she expected, and she ended up doing most of the work herself. Carlos knew she would handle the work well, but was afraid Peggy would say no. The parish's newcomer welcoming packet, including the names of current committee chairs, is due at the printer on Monday.

If you were Carlos, what would you do?

❑ Forget Peggy and look for someone else right away.
❑ Call Peggy to remind her how much the parish is counting on her.
❑ Just put her name down and hope she doesn't object.
❑ Start looking for a backup person, but meet with Peggy soon to help her discern whether the leadership role is right for her.

Peggy realizes that, if she is going to be effective, she needs to agree for the right reasons. Carlos can help her discover whether that is the case by helping her listen carefully to the messages in her head when she considers taking the position.

If Peggy hears herself saying any of the following, she should proceed with caution.

• Someone who knows what they are doing should take over.
• The whole parish will suffer if I don't agree to do this.
• If you want something done right, do it yourself.
• No one else wants the job.
• It annoys me that more people won't help.
• Work with other groups? That just makes things more complicated.
• We're well organized. There won't be that much to do, especially if we don't have to train any newcomers.
• Committee work and my spiritual life are separate things.
• The mission statement? It's on a plaque on the wall.

On the other hand, if Peggy agrees with most of the statements below, she may be ready to be a chairperson again.

• I understand the mission of the parish and how this group helps meet that mission.
• I have expertise in this area, but I want to learn more.
• I can explain how working with this committee can help me and others grow spiritually.
• Working effectively with the people on this committee is more important to me than getting the job done perfectly.
• I welcome newcomers and can help them become integral members of our team.
• I am willing to ask for help from others.

- I am willing to let go of expectations.
- This job might be fun!

In talking it through with Carlos, Peggy couldn't say yes to every item, especially the one about letting go of expectations, but she realized she had come a long way since here earlier experience. She agreed to give the role of chairperson one more try.

Do We Need a Handbook?

Preparing a handbook for parish volunteers may not be an exciting task, but it is helpful. A volunteer handbook ensures that essential information is distributed consistently. It gives volunteers an opportunity to learn more about the parish's vision, mission, and values and how their work as volunteers helps the parish move toward its goals. Most important, it lets volunteers know that their work is taken seriously.

As a bonus, preparing a volunteer handbook forces one or more parish leaders to examine volunteer ministry from a broad perspective, clarify expectations, come to terms with how staff and volunteers interact, and ensure compliance with legal mandates such as background checks for volunteers who work with youth.

What goes inside?

When it comes to content, the challenge is to balance what you want to put in with what volunteers are willing to read.

Professional volunteer managers advise basing content on your objectives. What information do you want every parish volunteer to know? What questions do new volunteers have? What questions do seasoned volunteers raise again and again? What problems seem to arise most often?

A volunteer handbook can include things like:

- a brief history of the parish
- a statement about its mission, vision, and goals
- an explanation of relevant parish policies
- personal stories that show volunteering as part of one's spiritual journey
- a complete list of volunteer opportunities
- safety procedures
- position descriptions
- confidentiality guidelines
- a flow chart of the parish to help volunteers understand

- who is accountable for what
- basics such as where to sign in, store coats and valuables, arrange for substitutes, and so on

Plan Format Upfront

Before you write a word, however, think about format. If it's going to be used, a volunteer handbook needs to be simple, organized, and concise. Will it need to be mailable? Will the handbook double as an orientation resource? Should it be flexible enough to allow for annual changes? Be printed in more than one language?

Plan for Distribution

Consider how you will distribute the handbook. Will every volunteer receive a copy? Will they be made available where volunteers check in? At orientations? Recognition events? Will they be mailed? e-mailed? Reproduced on audio- or videotape?

Write and Design

With key questions about content, format, and distribution answered, you are ready to write. Once the words say what you mean, use desktop publishing to create a pleasant arrangement of text on the page. Add white space and clip art to help readers find what they are looking for easily and keep interest levels high.

Seek Feedback

Most handbooks are "works in progress." Ask for suggestions on how to do yours better next time.

CHAPTER EIGHT

Lighting the Way

For the third night this week, Nate drove home from a parish meeting churning inside. With no official word from diocesan offices, merger speculations continued. Meetings, especially those involving collaboration between people from Saints Alive and Crosstown parishes, were marked by exaggerated courtesies designed to mask tensions bubbling just beneath the surface.

The joint liturgy committee had been among those most affected. Though she had agreed to help work out pulpit and choir exchanges, Saints Alive's new music director not only insisted that the parish start raising funds for a new organ, she had pretty much taken over all responsibility for preparing liturgy. In the interest of efficiency, she eliminated seasonal preparation teams, preferring to work with a select group of four people she called "helpers." Only one, however, was from Crosstown. She did agree to "wait and see" about continuing the liturgy-related study sessions but, since few people would ever become part of her team, attendance was dropping. Dan had shared his frustration in the volunteer ministry planning group's last three meetings.

Moreover, the diocese had made a consultant available to help Saints Alive bring its worship spaces up to date, and, in spite of ongoing arguments over the need for a new organ, remodeling was already under way. No similar arrangements were being made at Crosstown parish—a fact that did not go unnoticed by Rosa and her neighbors.

"It's clear they intend to shut us down," she had said at more than one meeting.

Still Nate was pleased that much of what the volunteer ministry planners had initiated also promoted collaboration. Now emphasizing hospitality, volunteers in the parish office seemed livelier, friendlier. Marge Landowski was relieved to find that the practice of ongoing recruitment meant she did not have to be solely responsible for maintaining a volunteer database. In fact, after meeting with Rosa, Marge had challenged her own assumptions and launched an inter-parish office volunteer exchange. The two women developed a plan through which volunteers from Crosstown could learn to use Saints Alive's computers and software for their own parish records in exchange for working in the Saints Alive office. Volunteers from Saints Alive could learn Spanish in exchange for volunteering in the Crosstown office. While pregnant with her first child, Cheryl had worked with Adele to arrange transportation and child care for volunteers at both sites.

Religious education classes now included children and teachers from both parishes. Rosa's son Ramon, who had uncovered an interest in teaching through the career planning office at the community college, was testing his talent by helping to prepare children for first Communion.

Roberto had taken several continuing education classes at a nearby seminary and had formed a multi-cultural Bible study group for adults. Casey and Harold had convinced Bill to support funding for a volunteer-oriented newsletter that would be printed in three languages. Last year, since Crosstown couldn't support a fund-raising festival of its own, the volunteer ministry planning group had suggested combining forces. Bill and Janet had been predictably skeptical but agreed that, if Crosstown parishioners contributed a certain number of volunteer hours, their parish would receive a percentage of the profits. The idea worked so well that the parish councils challenged both parishes to become full-scale partners for this year's event.

The approach had seemed a winning arrangement; but bickering erupted at the first planning meeting, and then escalated at the other committees on which festival planners served. Tonight, even people in the group that consciously practiced hospitality, studied discipleship, and worked unceasingly to build community, succumbed to merger madness. Nate could still hear the argument.

"The last thing you need here is an expensive new organ," Rosa said.

"It wasn't just our idea," said Janet. "Our new music director insisted."

Rosa retorted. "At Crosstown, we can't afford a music director."

"We can't afford any staff," Roberto added. "We're one of the poorest parishes in the diocese, so we do everything ourselves. That's why I come here. It isn't easy for me because I still don't feel I belong. But I keep coming. And I keep taking classes. So I can learn better what to do."

"Giving your parish half of what we earn at the festival isn't going to change that," Bill said.

"Shouldn't this discussion be happening at the festival committee meeting?" Harold asked.

"It did," Janet said. "We decided on a 70/30 split."

"We didn't decide on anything," Rosa said. "We discussed 70/30, 60/40, and 50/50; but we didn't decide. Then when the meeting notes came in the mail, they said we'd agreed on 70/30, and they didn't say anything about some of our other ideas to add more ethnic food booths and entertainment."

"We agreed to let Roberto make fresh tortillas," Janet said. "I'm not sure people here are interested in a mariachi band or Native American drumming."

"At the meeting you sounded as if you were all for it," argued Rosa.

"What else could I say?" Janet asked. "You kept pushing."

"Why did you agree to do things that way then?"

"Look, Rosa. If that merger comes through, we here at Saints Alive are going to have to do everything we can to make you feel welcome at our parish. We're going to have to let you folks do things your way a lot in the beginning if we are going to get along."

"*Let* us? Make us feel welcome at *your* parish? Is that what this group has been about, Nate?" Rosa's face was on fire.

"You know better than that," Nate had said but, as an African-American and a former member of Crosstown, he clearly understood how Rosa felt. "Harold's right. This isn't the appropriate meeting for this discussion. Let's get down to business."

The group tried, but found it impossible to agree on anything. Dan suggested developing a process for conflict resolution but no one supported his proposal except Glenna who said they should also consider a plan for conciliation. Casey asked for ideas on how to improve his newsletter, but everyone said it was fine.

Easing into his driveway, Nate was still concerned. After almost four years of his—their—hard work, the volunteer ministry planning group seemed to have reached its limits. Problems were clearly developing between staff and volunteers as well as among the volunteers themselves. Festival issues were only the beginning. Nate knew from experience that, as more collaborative efforts came down to the money issue, serious conflicts would arise. Worse, Nate wouldn't even be at the festival next month to do damage control because his oldest son was getting married in another state.

As soon as he walked through the kitchen door, Nate knew what he needed to do. He called Dan, then Glenna, and asked them if they would still be willing to draw up a process for conflict resolution and conciliation that would work with parish-centered volunteers.

Causes of Conflict

Wherever two or more are gathered, even in Jesus' name, conflict is eventually as inevitable as love. The situation above raises several of the many issues that bring conflict to life in parish settings:

- ambiguity (about impending changes, who is in charge, what overall goals are, and so on)
- "outsiders" (consultants, new staff, new committee chairs, even bishops, and so on) setting changes in motion
- differences of opinion (over values, priorities, timing, and so forth)
- assuming "discussion" = "decision"
- one-up/one-down relationships (staff over volunteers, volunteers over staff, chairpersons over groups, longstanding members over newcomers, "big" parish over "little" parish, and so on)
- underlying power delineators (racism, sexism, economic disadvantage, physical disabilities)

Write other conflict-generators that you have observed or experienced in your parish on a separate sheet of paper.

Like other aspects of management, approaches to conflict tend to match the management model from which an organization operates. When farm-based models prevailed, independent individuals worked out their own conflicts (or not) without expecting help from the community. Traditional industrial management models, with their emphasis on "one best way" and hierarchical structures, relied on one-up/everyone else down relationships. Because uneducated, easily replaceable workers needed jobs to survive, "like it or leave" approaches to conflict were common. In parish life, the voices of the pastor and his closest advisors most often prevailed in conflict situations.

As factory-based models evolved and trained workers were seen as harder-to-replace parts of complex machines, dialogue became a component of conflict resolution, but the "playing field" was still uneven. Skilled managers learned to negotiate, but had the power to fall back on coercion or manipulation if sincere dialogue didn't produce the desired results. Post-Vatican II parish life also promoted dialogue as a component of conflict resolution but, as in the rest of the organizational world, the playing field remained uneven. In some cases, misunderstandings about power and what dialogue could accomplish generated conflict that deeply affected parish-centered volunteers.

The process models of the late twentieth century emphasized worker empowerment, horizontal structures, and win/win solutions for people in conflict in "learning organizations." Managers learned to integrate healing and conciliation practices into organizational life. Though in parishes it is still not unusual to hear someone say, "We should all get along...this is the Church!" many of today's parish-centered volunteers can see the benefit of incorporating similar practices into parish life.

A Question of Power

Power is always a factor in organizational life. Leaders may deliberate about how power *could* be distributed and/or take on the challenge of redistributing power as they think it *should* be distributed. Managers, however, are expected to bring out the best in the power that *is*. The question managers can fairly ask about power is not "how can I (or my committee or group) get more of it in this organization?" but "what kind of environment is resulting from how we use the power I (we) do have—an environment characterized by fear? or by trust?"

On a separate sheet of paper, describe the environment of your parish as it relates to power.

> Quick Tip: Some conflict in parish life is related to "big picture" issues. As an individual, you have the right and responsibility to give voice to and even take the lead in promoting your position in appropriate ways and in appropriate settings.
>
> When you put on your "manager" hat, however, you agree to support the current system and operate within its structures. You are accountable for leading your committee or group in developing and implementing objectives that support the stated goals and plans established by those who set direction for the parish, for fulfilling the stated mission, and for moving toward the stated vision. If you are uncomfortable with doing that, this may not be the best time for you to be in a management role. It is not OK to manage parish resources in ways that promote a personal or group agenda that does not match the stated agenda of the community.

In organizations where trust prevails, you are likely to find that everything matches. People match their thoughts, words, and actions to what they truly believe. Even when people are unhappy with decisions made by those with power, the resulting consistency and clarity lead to an ever-increasing level of trust and strong relationships characterized by mutual respect for the others' integrity.

In organizations where fear prevails, people tend to think (or pretend to think) what others want them to think, say and do what others want them to say and do, or say one thing and do another. Even when people see that a particular conflicted situation is going their way, the resulting ambiguity leads to an ever-increasing level of mistrust or fear about those with power. People with little power worry about losing what they do have and those with much power worry about competing for more. Since most volunteers hesitate to confront authorities in a church setting, their fear is most often expressed as anger, sadness, frustration, withholding, indifference, or total detachment.

Consider some of the issues raised at the volunteer ministry planning group meeting. For each of the following issues, use one of the codes listed below to describe what volunteers are likely to feel in response to this action.

HT: High level of trust
ST: Somewhat trustful
SF: Somewhat fearful
HF: High level of fear

_____ Rumors circulate about an impending merger.

_____ Paid staff member reverses an important decision made by volunteers.

_____ New staff assumes full authority in an area previously managed well by volunteers.

_____ An "outsider" manages a major change.

_____ An administrative assistant initiates changes that serve the needs of volunteers.

_____ A manager seems willing to experiment with new ideas.

_____ Funds are made available for a project that serves parish-centered volunteers.

_____ Group members argue at length over issues that are not part of their meeting agenda.

_____ A decision is publicized before the group reaches consensus.

_____ Volunteers believe that permission from paid staff is always needed to move forward with a worthwhile idea.

_____ Volunteers know that a process is in place for resolving conflicts.

_____ A conflict generator is observed or experienced at your parish.

A person who manages parish-centered volunteers may not have power in situations such as those above, but keeping the trust/fear continuum in mind can help you better serve volunteers involved in the conflict. As a manager, instead of pointing them to "just move on" solutions, you can light the way to community-strengthening options. Whatever the situation, a first step is to guide volunteers in exploring their own version of the power question: Not "How can we get more power in the situation?" but "In this situation, how can we use the power we *do* have to create an environment characterized by trust?"

Parishes pay a high price for assuming a "this shouldn't happen here" or a "let's move on" approach to managing conflict that involves volunteers. Most often managers who use those approaches mean well. They don't realize that taking the easy way out in the sort term negatively affects the long term. Unresolved conflict:

- severely limits what can be accomplished because it creates a grouping of "undiscussables"
- limits the potential for community because it offers no way to deal with barriers to strong relationships
- reduces the commitment level of potentially dedicated volunteers

Because only a handful of volunteers will push hard on difficult issues, the people who manage them rarely see the cracks forming in volunteer commitment levels until it is too late. "Damage control" may be enough to keep those volunteers on board for the short term but, unless the issues that produced the conflicts for them are fairly and fully addressed, fearful (angry, sad, frustrated, withdrawn, indifferent, detached) volunteers are unlikely to continue investing their energies in parish-centered work. Having processes in place for conflict resolution and conciliation can go a long way toward promoting strong, healthy relationships among volunteers as well as between volunteers and your parish as a whole.

> Quick Tip: Be honest. If you think that developing a formal process for conflict resolution in your parish will result in little more than giving lip service to the idea, trust your instincts. Just don't let that attitude hamper your own ability to manage well. Many people who manage parish volunteers are not in a position to implement parish-wide changes. But you can choose to practice conflict resolution and conciliation in your own arena of influence.

If you are managing from a discipleship model, strong, healthy relationships are already developing between you and parish-centered volunteers because you are working as a disciple in the company of disciples. Though you respect the authority that emanates from legitimate power bases within your parish system, you also remain open to the power that emanates from the work of the Holy Spirit in your own arena of influence. You see conflict management as more than promoting win/lose or even win/win results so the group can move on. Instead you see conflict management as a win/learn situation that relies on the guidance of the Holy Spirit to produce the best possible short-term result while pursuing wisdom that will enrich your parish's long-term journey.

Volunteer Ministry Planner 8: Resolve Conflict to Strengthen Healthy Relationships

Step 1: Be sure your committee or group has a clear purpose and that every member of your group is willing to be held accountable for fulfilling that purpose. If you haven't already done so, spend time at one of your meetings answering the following questions:

- What is our overall purpose?
- What work does the parish expect us to accomplish? How will we go about doing that work?
- In addition to what the parish expects, for what else will we hold ourselves accountable?
- What help will we need? How will we go about getting that help?
- How will we make decisions as a group?
- How will we solve problems as a group?
- How will we communicate with each other? with others in the parish?
- When, how, will we invite guidance from the Holy Spirit?

Step 2: Agree that conflict resolution and conciliation are important to the success of the group. Many people are so uncomfortable with conflict they will do anything to avoid dealing with it. Especially if one person is perceived to have more authority than the rest of the group members (a priest or deacon, a staff member, the chairperson, a member who also serves with the parish council, a long-time member, and so on), many people are likely to turn their power over to that person and expect them to resolve any conflicts that arise.

Step 3: Design a process for conflict resolution.

- *Invite all stakeholders to participate.* Be sure all participants know when and where sessions will take place and have copies of all relevant materials.
- *Select a facilitator.* Someone who is not a stakeholder should facilitate the process.

Quick Tip: Add "prospect for facilitators" to your to-do list. Effective twenty-first century managers will develop a team of people who have or are willing to learn facilitation skills and prepare them for parish-specific conflict resolution.

- *Gather in a spirit of hospitality and discipleship.* Be prepared to welcome and learn from everyone present.
- *Agree on/amend facilitator-developed guidelines.* The facilitator will have thought through guidelines that serve most groups well. Each group is accountable for agreeing on guidelines that are likely to work well for them before they begin working on the conflict itself. Though not ideal, if the group can't agree, the facilitator can impose guidelines to get the process off the ground.
- *Listen to issues as they are presented without interruption by both sides.*
- *Identify areas of agreement.*
- *Clarify which areas are still in conflict.*
- *Decide whether more information is needed.* Assign responsibility for bringing more information to the group. The first session may need to end at this point. Decide on a date and time to reconvene when the necessary information will be available.
- *With all needed information in place, read your parish mission statement aloud.* Discuss how the information presented and the issue in question relate to the parish's overall mission.
- *Propose solutions.* The facilitator calls for proposals from either side and guides the group in determining how each proposal will further the mission of the parish.
- *Pray.* If you haven't already done so, invite the Holy Spirit to get involved in the process.
- *Reach consensus.* Choose the proposal that provides satisfactory resolution for all stakeholders and best serves the mission of the parish. You may schedule additional sessions to achieve consensus.

Hint: Coming to consensus doesn't mean that everyone has to agree. Consensus is reached when all stakeholders agree not to stand in the way of a implementing the solution that most see as best for the community.

- *Celebrate community.* If emotions ran deep or some stakeholder felt seriously wounded, celebration may not be immediate. There may be a need to practice forgiveness first. That can take time. Meanwhile, celebrate how the conflict resolution process strengthened the sense of community among participants. Celebrate belief in God's healing power. Celebrate willingness to forgive even if forgiveness itself doesn't seem likely.

Complete forgiveness involves acknowledging that we have been hurt and that life changed for the worse as a result of that hurt. It involves acknowledging that we may have also hurt others, that we need forgiveness too. It involves becoming willing to forgive and to be forgiven; then, when we are ready, taking whatever action we need to take to offer and seek forgiveness. It involves making amends to those whom we have hurt and expecting that, through the forgiveness process, our lives will change for the better. Finally it involves celebrating freedom from pain and the stronger sense of relationship that may have evolved through the process.

Volunteers from Saints Alive and Crosstown parishes were busy preparing for the final day of the festival. The Friday night and Saturday events had drawn predictable crowds. Sunday was traditionally the biggest attendance day and the early morning radio forecast nothing but sunshine. Families were already spilling over from the outdoor Mass, lured by the savory aroma of sizzling chicken.

Bill's crew had fired up the grills by 9:30 that morning. Several dozen cooked quarters were already warming in huge ovens while more roasted crisp and juicy over hot coals. In the cafeteria, the caterer was cutting up three hundred more that he'd thawed overnight on refrigerator shelves.

They felt the cloud before they actually saw it. Wind chimes in the arts and crafts booth sang just a bit faster. The inflated tumbling walk cast just a bit more shadow. Joshua Alexander ran over from the swing set, dusted with sand. "Mom, look!" He pointed to the western sky as a chill puff of black circled over the parish grounds.

Janet shivered and bit her lip. "It will blow over," she said.

But the darkness slid forward and settled into place. Big drops of rain splashed onto the grills, rising up in steam. An older couple hurriedly retreated to the parking lot. The rain fell heavier now; the festival grounds were shrouded in darkness. Light sensitive spotlamps flickered on, sparked, and fizzled dark again. The rain was heavy now and, as the lightning flashed soundlessly nearby, Bill could see that the coals had just about been doused.

What frightened Janet most was the intensity of the wind. She watched spellbound as it lifted one side of the big tent and held it vertical over the canopy. Families streamed away from the outdoor Mass. Everywhere she looked, volunteers in game booths were frantically scooping prizes into boxes. Someone must have moved a rock weighing down napkins in the food tent because paper squares flew every which way. The musicians hastily packed up their instruments and fled to their van.

The next gust took the back pole of the bingo tent. Janet watched the canvas collapse forward, drenched by the weight of the rain.

"Come on," Rosa yelled. "Let everything go. Get inside."

Janet ran across the parking lot where Rosa struggled to hold the church door open for her. Several dozen volunteers watched helplessly as the wind played with the carnival games for several minutes, dumped barrels of rain over the pink flesh of the half-cooked chickens, and moved on.

The festival grounds were deserted. One by one, volunteers emerged from their shelters into a steady downpour. Not a speck of sun was visible.

"Maybe it will clear up later," Rosa said half-heartedly.

"No," said Bill. "Festival's over. Let's clean up and go home."

Adele brought a carton of trash bags from the cafeteria and the group began retrieving soggy prizes from the puddles forming on the asphalt. The caterer dumped the ruined chickens and soggy coals into big garbage barrels, then handed Janet the bill.

"Don't know what you can do with the rest in the kitchen," he said. "It's no good trying to freeze them again."

Casey was the first to notice that Joshua Alexander was missing. Not wanting to alarm Glenna, he took a quick run around the entire property. He found the boy with Roberto on the other side of the building. Under the sheltered drop-off area in front of the church, Roberto had fired up his tortilla grill and was whisking water into the masa.

"I mixed up a couple of batches early," he said. "We might as well use it up as throw it out."

When a few drops of cool water danced on the surface, he carefully ladled the first spoonful of batter onto the hot griddle and watched it fill with air.

"Hmm," said Joshua Alexander as the smell of fresh flatbread escaped from under the overhang.

Casey went to get the others but they were already moving toward the enticing aroma. The volunteers lined up as, one by one, Roberto served up the breads. Exhausted, Janet had sunk down on the ground next to a pillar. Rosa carried a warm tortilla over to her.

"It's too bad things didn't work out," she said. "If you keep all the profits, you might still have made enough to get that organ though."

Janet folded her hands around the warm tortilla and smiled. "Thanks, Rosa," she said, "but we had a deal. The organ will have to wait."

Practical Matters 8

Into the Fire

Pick one of the following situations described in Chapter 8 (or a situation you have observed or experienced in your own parish). Work through the conflict resolution process below applying it to the specific situation. Use the format that follows and write your thoughts on a separate piece of paper.

Conflict Situation A: Some liturgy committee volunteers do not like the way the new music director has re-organized liturgy preparation work.

Conflict Situation B: Rumors continue to circulate about the possibility of a merger between Crosstown and Saints Alive parishes.

Conflict Situation C: People on the festival committee disagree about several issues.

Conflict Situation D: Tension is mounting in the volunteer ministry planning group.

Conflict Situation E (selected from your own parish): _____

Step 1: Describe in full the situation where the conflict has arisen. Be as objective as possible.

    A. List Side A's position
    B. List Side B's position
    C. List Side C's position

Step 2: Invite all stakeholders to participate.

    List all who have a stake in the outcome of the situation by name or by role in the parish, whichever seems more appropriate. Does our situation also involve stakeholders who are not part of the parish? If so, put them on the list.

What materials will stakeholders need to prepare for effective conflict resolution?

When/where will sessions take place?

How will all participants be notified?

Step 3: Select a facilitator.

Who has the skills, is willing, and is available to serve as our facilitator?

Step 4: Gather in a spirit of hospitality and discipleship.

How will we prepare the room to be as welcoming as possible?

How will people be welcomed to the sessions?

How will session organizers inspire a sense of discipleship?

Step 5: Agree on/amend facilitator-developed guidelines.

What guidelines do we need to facilitate discussion in general?

What guidelines will we need to facilitate discussion about this situation?

Step 6: Listen to issues as they are presented without interruption by both sides.

How will we ensure that participants listen to each side without interrupting?

How much time will each side be given to present their issues?

What issues do we expect to surface from Side A? Side B? Side C?

Step 7: Identify areas of agreement.

On what do we expect participants to agree?

How can we best affirm their agreements?

CHAPTER NINE

Fired Up!

When Abuela died late in March, Crosstown parish church was filled with people. Many were long-time friends and relatives of Abuela, Rosa, and her husband Mike. Others were new friends from Saints Alive who came to pray with the family.

Adele and Harold, sporting rugged tans from a two-month stint building houses in El Salvador, sat just behind Cheryl and Doug. Cheryl was pregnant again, this time with twins. She had already announced that, except for helping with the young mom's group, she wouldn't be doing much volunteering until all three little ones started school.

Casey had taken a job on the coast. The moving van had already left with his belongings but, when he heard about Abuela, he decided to postpone his own departure until after the funeral. Glenna was still reeling from the pain of becoming single again but, praying there with her children, she appeared stronger and more confident than ever. Bill, of all people, when he heard that Glenna had no family in the area, had taken on an almost grandfatherly role. As he and Janet slipped into the pew in front of Glenna and her family, he and Josh exchanged a subdued high-five.

Rosa and Mike had asked Nate to preside and Nate had asked Dan to assist. As the prayer service drew to a close, Nate asked if anyone had a story to tell about Abuela. At first, relatives and friends came forward relating stories, sometimes moving, sometimes funny, about the gift Abuela had been in their lives.

Eventually Bill walked to the ambo.

Bill's Story

"I'm not from the family and I'm not from this parish, but I have something I want to tell you about Abuela and me," he said. "I didn't know her well, but she is the reason I have decided to explore a whole new career. Though I saw Abuela every couple of months for the last few years, we never really spoke. In fact, it occurred to me when I thought about what I would say today, that I'd never actually heard her voice. To be honest, most of the time, I resented her being at our meetings. She never really contributed anything, but she had a way of letting us, especially me, know when she disapproved of something.

"Some years ago, we started to try different approaches to recruiting volunteers at our parish. One thing we did was, when we used a printed form, we offered open-ended options instead of just asking people to check off specific activities. One of the options was, "I am unable to help the parish in any of the ways you have suggested above, but I will pray for the parish." I didn't like the idea, but I was overruled.

"Last spring, since we were planning a joint festival, we used a printed form at Saints Alive and sent the same form to you here at Crosstown. Normally, I'm not one of the people who reads the responses but, since my wife and I were recruiting volunteers for the festival, they gave us the forms to go through first. One of them really stood out. I don't have it with me, but I have not forgotten what the person who sent it back wrote. It went like this:

Thank you for asking me to help. When I was a young woman, I was very active in the parish. I started volunteering while my children were in the parish school and, even after they left home, I served on a lot of different parish committees. For the last ten years though, I have had to let go of a lot of things, my activities, my friends, even my home. I needed help from my children and grandchildren just to get to Mass. Now I am homebound. I feel bad that there isn't a way I can help at church anymore.

But I can pray and I do pray for the parish so I am returning this card to let you know that. Thank you for letting me know that what I can do for the parish counts for something.

"The letter was signed 'Maria Martinez.' One more time Abuela had touched my life.

"A famous composer said that too many people die with their music still in them. Abuela didn't do that, but I am afraid that many people in our parishes do. We plan and we do; we ask for opinions and help; we even pray. We dance to the rhythm of our own agendas, but we never really listen for the music among the silent.

"Not me. No more. I will never again be able to attend a parish meeting without hearing Abuela there. Her silence is a powerful sound to me now, a symphony of elderly, homebound, lonely, different, indifferent, fallen away, questioning people of God—all the people I used to think didn't get it. I thought they all needed to change if our parish was to be better and that they needed me to get them to do that.

"All along, it was me who didn't get it, me who needs to change, who needs to listen for the music in everyone no matter how softly it plays...."

Bill stopped talking when his voice started to crack. When he returned to his pew, the boy behind him stood on the kneeler and patted Bill hard on his shoulder. "Way to go," said Joshua Alexander. "Good story!"

No matter how bogged down we get with day-to-day parish demands, we have one "good story" to tell. It's a story about change, a resurrection story, and it happens again and again. It happens to the ordained. It happens to lay ministry professionals. And it happens to volunteers.

How nice it would be if, having recruited all the volunteers we need, we could freeze them in the moment. Even if they learned something new, strengthened their skills, even if their lives kicked into overdrive, even if their faith suddenly started bubbling over, the freeze-frame folks would stand firm to their volunteer commitments. We would never have to think much about them again. Instead we could just pick up the phone and call the volunteer we need.

Need publicity? Call Mary. Someone to make phone calls? Get Betty. George is the guy with the truck. Rolf takes money to the bank. Naryan hands out groceries from the food pantry. Count on Gert to put on after-dinner funeral receptions. How clean! How simple! How unlike the story we tell.

In truth, if we are managing volunteers well, existing gifts will strengthen; new gifts will emerge. If we have been good stewards, most volunteers will grow into change. They will need to try new experiences or relive old experiences in new ways. Ready or not, those changes will affect parish-centered volunteer ministry.

Why Promote Movement in Ministry?

In any organization, a manager expects to bring out the best in its human resources in order to reach the organization's goals, an appropriate role for managers of parish-centered volunteers as well. In a Spirit-driven organization, however, change among God's people is one of the goals. The community and individuals within it strive for ongoing conversion. People who manage parish volunteers expect to bring out the best in volunteers, not only for the good of the organization but for the good of individuals within it. Moving in volunteer ministry is one way to accomplish that.

Had Bill restricted his volunteer work to the finance committee, for example, he would have continued to contribute to the good of the parish. Participating in the volunteer ministry planning group, however, brought out a gift of empathy he hadn't realized was there. Having discovered that gift, it will be difficult for Bill to operate in the way he had before. He will have to discern new ways of contributing to the parish that integrate all of his gifts. Effective managers will plan to involve volunteers in an ongoing process of discovery and discernment.

Moving in Ministry

We have considered well-written job/project descriptions, careful matching of volunteers with work, and striving for retention as critical tools for effective volunteer management. In a Spirit-driven organization, however, there is another step to take. Instead of using those tools to develop done-deal, dead-end destinations for volunteers, use them as springboards to other opportunities. When a term of service concludes, volunteers who see themselves as disciples have several personally beneficial options, each of which also benefits the parish.

- *They can return for another term in the same position.* Returning is the most common choice. When done thoughtfully, returning benefits the parish by bringing more experience to the work. When managing from the perspective of discipleship, however, encourage volunteers to consider whether they still have more to learn in that role. If not, it may be time for change.
- *They can continue in the same role, but do things differently.* The return-but-adapt approach can bring new ideas and experience together in ways that benefit the individual as well as the parish.
- *They can move into a leadership position.* Experienced volunteers with energy and commitment are truly beneficial to the parish. Be sure they have plenty of training and support, as well as a gracious way to step out, rather than burn-out, of a leadership role. You can help volunteers recognize their readiness for leadership by helping them explore some questions:

> *Do I share the vision for our parish and understand its mission?*
> *Do I understand how parish values evolve from Scripture and tradition?*
> *Am I comfortable with the art of reflection?*
> *Am I willing to make mistakes, even risk failure?*
> *Do I tend to match my words and actions with my beliefs?*
> *Am I hungry for some really challenging experiences?*
> *Am I resilient?*
> *Does my life have room for increased commitments?*
> *Am I willing to help bring out the best in others?*

- *They can start over in a different ministry.* Though it appears the parish is losing the volunteer's experience, it actually benefits from the change. The volunteer brings that experience to the new area of ministry, broadening everyone's insights into the overall work of the parish.

- *They can move into formation, faith-sharing, or support groups.* People volunteer informally at all stages of their life-cycle. When formal volunteering is not feasible, the parish benefits by giving back, by making life-generating opportunities available and valuing the informal volunteering that takes place within them.

- *They can move to ministry outside of parish boundaries.* The parish benefits by becoming more connected to the global community as well as by being enriched by the insights and experiences global volunteers bring to the faith community.

- *They can move into formal preparation for professional ministry.* Many people currently working in paid positions in parishes heard the call to professional ministry while serving as volunteers. It makes sense to make materials available from seminaries and universities that prepare adults for ecclesial lay ministry rather than assuming such a call is unlikely to surface among volunteers.

Hint: One reason it is so difficult to explore the topic of moving in ministry is confusion over whether the word "ministry" is appropriate when referring to non-commissioned people who volunteer or whether the word "volunteer" is appropriate when referring to people who are living out a baptismal call.

It's time to bring that debate to a close. Whether responding to their baptismal call, a notice in the bulletin, or an SOS from a friend, most people understand the term "volunteer" to mean someone who is not receiving monetary compensation for a service they provide. They can tell the difference between completing a task and carrying out the trust of ministry. They know that, in parish life, both tasks and ministry are accomplished by both paid staff and volunteers. They also know that, when an organization intends to help people encounter Christ, all people in all roles within it are of enormous value. It's not the word "volunteer" that bothers them; it's the diminishing "non"-sense we attach to the term.

"My garden is full of beautiful perennials and lots of them are 'volunteers,' delightful surprises that crop up in places I never planted them," Adele said. "None of them are non-flowers. Please don't ask me to think of myself as a non-paid, non-ordained, non-ecclesial lay minister. Let me bloom where the Spirit planted me. I'm a volunteer!"

Volunteer Ministry Planner 9: Facilitate Movement

As volunteers grow in faith and experience, their individual interests are bound to change. As the faith community absorbs the experiences of these developing disciples, parish interests are bound to change. The changes will be reflected in the vision, mission, and strategies of those who set direction for your parish. As an effective manager, you will see movement in volunteer ministry as both the cause and consequence of those changes. Instead of planning one project or one year at a time, it helps to integrate moving in ministry into your overall plan for parish-centered volunteers.

Anticipate Changes

Review your vision and purpose statements on page 20. How does encouraging volunteers to move in ministry support your vision?

Your purpose?

_____

_____

_____

Name three important goals from your parish's long-range plan or one-year plan.

_____

_____

_____

How will your group help the parish meet those goals over the next twenty-four months?

_____

_____

_____

How many additional volunteers will you need to accomplish those objectives?

_____

Will everyone currently in your group remain for the entire two years?

_____

How many additional volunteers will you need to replace those who might leave?

_____

Are you likely to experience a change in leadership?   ___ Yes ___ No

If so, talk about and prepare for it now. When the time comes to make that change, it won't seem so frightening. "What will I have to do?" will already be spelled out.

Practice Discernment

Getting comfortable with group discernment when making important decisions helps people increase their comfort level with the practice of individual discernment. Discernment draws on an understanding of facts without limiting itself to factual answers, considers varied opinions, and invites God into the process of decision-making.

Instead of just reacting to "we think you're the best person for the job" or "we really need someone and no one else is available" statements, volunteers take many factors into account when deciding their future with a group. Discernment opens individuals and the group up to risk because they can no longer assume things won't change. Instead they gather relevant information from each other about position, work, family, and time commitments as well as about interests and needs. They listen to each other, reflect on what they learn, and plan ahead for changes.

Spot and Nurture Leadership Qualities

Instead of assuming that the same person will always be there to lead, the group helps everyone develop personal leadership skills. Effective group leaders are:

- *Learners.* They respect committee history and procedures, but remain ever open to new people, new ideas, and new ways of doing things.
- *Evaluators.* Effective leaders set aside time in every meeting to evaluate how the group's current work serves the mission of the parish and adjust plans whenever necessary.

- *Affirmers.* Effective leaders affirm not just what gets done but how it gets done. They understand that the most important work of the group is to sustain an environment in which each member can grow in faith.
- *Discoverers.* Effective leaders are quick to recognize how the Holy Spirit is working in a group and make that known.

Let Go

Effective managers of parish-centered volunteers see the "career path" of a volunteer as the lifelong journey of a disciple. Moving in and out of formal volunteer ministry, the disciple continues responding to his or her baptismal call through informal ministry, both giving to and receiving from God's people who share this leg of that journey.

Simon's Story

Born the son of Jonah, I settled in Capharnaum and developed a profitable fishing operation. My brother Andrew became interested in the preaching of the man who baptized people in the Jordan. When Andrew told me he had found the Messiah there, I was skeptical but curious. He took me to meet him and, before I knew what was happening, this man looked at me and said, "Thou shalt be called Cephas." (You know me as Peter.) Curious change.

Back at work, this man Jesus asked me to take him out in my boat one day. He told me, all of us, that instead of just catching fish, we would be "fishers of men." Interesting change.

After that, I found myself spending more and more time with Jesus. There were at least twelve of us that always seemed to be there, but he always seemed to be singling me out. Part of the reason, I guess, is because I was always doing rash things. One night, I saw Jesus walking on the water toward us in the boat. Next thing I knew, I was walking on water too. Of course, the minute I realized what was happening, I sank. In many ways, that was the story of my life. I had so much faith in this man. I loved him. I saw miracles happen in his presence. I learned from his stories. Then I'd do something that made it seem as if I didn't understand a thing about him. Inside, though, I felt myself changing. Exciting!

Over time, it became clear to me that he was the Messiah, the Son of the living God. I took on more and more responsibilities in the group. One day Jesus called me "Rock." He said he was entrusting me with the keys to the kingdom of heaven. Incredible change!

Eventually, though, they took him away. That's when I messed up big time. I thought it would be so easy, following him all the way. It wasn't. I failed. I let him down. I let myself down. Humbling change.

Then everything changed. So quickly! It was glorious, yet terrifying. The mistakes, the doubts, the fears didn't matter so much anymore. There was so much to tell, to share, to learn. We felt so unprepared; but all of us were transforming. We couldn't wait to get out there and tell the story in ways, in places, we'd never told it before. We were totally fired up!

Practical Matters 9

What Is the "Career Path" of a Volunteer?

Here is how one volunteer, Andy, described his:

It started with a longing for something I couldn't even name, just a nagging feeling that there was more I could be doing with my life. I started looking around for something that could quiet the feeling. Our company president is on the board of a non-profit agency, so I started taking part in, then organizing, fund-raisers for it. I tried a couple of other things too, mostly fund-raising activities, some at my parish.

One day someone invited me to get involved in our prison ministry. I don't know why I said yes. Just curious, I guess. One trip to the prison and I felt in my gut this was something I could feel good about doing. But I held back for a long time. Truthfully, I was scared—not just about working with prisoners. I knew that getting involved with prison ministry would be a long-term commitment and would require some attitude changes on my part.

I'd already taken the first step and responded to the invitation. I spent the next three years learning about the ministry, just volunteering every month or so; then three more years volunteering every week in the prison. I think I became a master at working with the system there. Then I spent the next three years teaching others what I'd learned so we could expand our ministry.

Now I'm ready to move on. Working with some of the prisoners who were dying has made me realize how to help people with that process. I'm studying now to become a chaplain. I'm not sure if I will stay with the prisons or do other kinds of chaplain work. I'll figure that out when the time is right.

Andy's story names several steps in his volunteer career path. Check the steps you currently address in plans for parish-centered volunteer ministry in your parish.

❑ recognizing the longing to do something worthwhile with one's life
❑ respecting/aiding the exploration process
❑ inviting specific involvement
❑ trusting "gut feel" instead of pushing for commitment
❑ providing opportunities to learn about a ministry
❑ respecting the universal desire to master certain areas of practice
❑ providing opportunities to teach others what one has learned
❑ encouraging the desire to move on
❑ facilitating discernment

Adding or improving on which of the above steps would be most likely to enhance what volunteers experience in your parish?
How?

Picture the volunteer you named on page 10. Which of the above steps would be most likely to enhance what he/she experiences as a volunteer in your parish?
How?

If you wanted to choose just one of the above steps to incorporate in your plans for parish-centered ministry now, which one would it be?
Why?

Will you do that? __ Yes __ No

When?

An Aid to Discernment

If volunteers are not sure whether to return to a ministry or move on to something else, this set of questions may help them decide.

- In my faith life, I have grown in the following practices:
- One practice in my faith life that is significantly different from last year at this time is:
- By next year at this time, I would like to have grown in the practice of:
- A current project that is helping me grow in faith is:
- It challenges me in the following ways:
- One thing I do to help me grow that no one knows about is:
- Things I have learned about life and God in the last year are:
- To grow in faith by this time next year, I might need help from:
- One thing I have hesitated to talk about in my role as a volunteer is:
- One thing I wish decision-makers here knew is:
- As a parish-centered volunteer, the best thing I could do next is:

For Practice: Helping Volunteers Decide

Gina chaired the human concerns committee for five years. Lately she feels drawn to learn more about prayer and worship. But whenever she thinks about moving into a new ministry, she worries. Who will take her place? How will they know what has to be done? What if the whole committee falls apart? What steps can Gina take that will help her decide what to do next? What questions could she ask herself?

Picture yourself as the staff person who works with the human concerns committee. What could you do to help Gina make her decision?

Picture yourself as the chair of the prayer and worship committee. What could you do to help Gina make her decision?

Burn-out Busting

Far too many parish-centered volunteers hang on too long before they let go of a commitment or move out of a ministry. The result can be burn-out, not at all what we pray for when we ask the Holy Spirit to send down the fire. How can you bust burn-out among volunteers once and for all?

- *Recognize symptoms.* Volunteers heading for burn-out will seem more irritable, tired, and resigned. They may stop coming to meetings or start coming late more often. They may contribute fewer ideas or talk about what's not working more than what is. When you talk with them, they may have a hard time putting a finger on what's wrong.
- *Redraw the map.* Instead of offering volunteer experiences that resemble rush hour on the freeway, redesign them as true spiritual journeys. With the first approach, recruits merge into a frenzy of activity, jockey for an effective position, grow weary and exit as soon as they find an off-ramp somewhere near their destination. Along the way, they miss the lights, sounds, and tastes of conversion. They catch a sense of unfolding mystery in increments, like in the old Burma shave messages, and spot miracles billboard-style as they speed by.

The second approach allows volunteers to spend more time on the frontage road, easing on and off when they are ready to drive forward or retreat. They take time to mark milestones, regroup at rest stops, reflect on scenic views, and stop immediately whenever they sense a need for repairs.

When it comes to burn-out, what applies to individuals also applies to groups. To stave off group burn-out, plan to do one of these activities at least once each calendar year.

- *Look through the window of opportunity*—try to see your parish as if you were seeing it for the first time…what can your group do differently to help create the parish you envision?
- *Pilot something;* don't wait for sure-thing proof that a new program is needed; put research on hold and try something out. If it doesn't work, let it go. If it needs improvement, adapt and pilot again.
- *Give yourself an imaginary unlimited budget.* Without changing your group's purpose, what could you do with more money? Dream a lot. Before you insist on coming back to reality, see if there isn't some fragment of your dream that could happen without having a lot more money. How can you help it happen?
- *Give yourselves permission to be real change leaders.* If all organizational roadblocks were removed, what really important project would your group take on? Though others may have low expectations for you as volunteers, you don't have to limit yourselves to uncreative assignments. The more volunteers settle for unchallenging work, the more others believe that that is all volunteers are capable of. The view of volunteers as low-level task completers

becomes a self-fulfilling prophecy. Be honest. What can your group accomplish that no other group in the parish is ready or able to do?

Do We Need a Volunteer Coordinator?

In both for- and non-profit sectors, the position of "volunteer coordinator" is becoming increasingly important. In the for-profit sector, a volunteer coordinator works out of the human resource or community relations departments, striving to expand company participation in the community by linking employees with volunteer opportunities in social service agencies. In the non-profit world, hiring a volunteer coordinator to increase recruitment and retention is seen as necessary for the organization's survival. In both cases, the volunteer coordinator's primary role is to involve people in fulfilling the goals of the organization.

In parish life, a volunteer coordinator's role is broader. When parishes see the benefits of creating the position of volunteer coordinator, they do so not just to fulfill its own goals but to facilitate the process of discipleship. More important than building recruitment and increasing retention, a volunteer coordinator in a discipling community helps people move in ministry.

Joan's Story

When I meet a new person at my parish now, I am "all ears." I'm a volunteer coordinator, a new position many believe is critical if a parish wants to benefit from the varied gifts of its parishioners. I've long been a committed volunteer and I was disappointed that some committees and parish events were just stagnating. They never seemed to have enough manpower or creative energy to do new things. Meanwhile other committees were overflowing with energy and creativity. The irony was hard to ignore.

On the one hand, here were things falling apart; on the other hand, here was all this energy coming in.

As a volunteer coordinator, I take a more personal approach, get to know new and old parishioners, find out what they enjoy doing. Then I match them up with volunteer jobs. I try to come up with creative ideas like putting "want ads" in our parish bulletin. One ad inviting gardeners to a Green Thumb festival got flowers planted and shrubs trimmed on parish grounds. We saw people there who had never volunteered before and others who hadn't volunteered in a long time. After the festival, some in the group organized a once-a-month gardening get together. Now they also contribute produce from their own gardens to a meal program.

Paid staff also began to realize the benefits of having a volunteer coordinator. Now they ask me to find them help for special projects. A box used to collect money for local food pantries, for example, wasn't producing enough cash to meet the parish's minimum commitment. I advertised for a creative team to design a marketing campaign. Their efforts were successful and took only a few hours of volunteer time.

Our council didn't want this to be a paid position, but they are rethinking that now that they are seeing results. We are starting to see a volunteer coordinator as a "creative opportunist." You take what you know about the parish and what you know about what people are interested in, bring them together, and see where it leads. We can't expect time/talent sheets or the pastor or parish secretary to do that. Someone needs to be dedicating time to this exclusively.

Some committee chairs were afraid that a volunteer coordinator would force them to take on new committee members or tell them how to do things. Since that didn't happen, even the skeptics came on board. People are beginning to realize that having a volunteer coordinator is a real benefit to the parish as well as to the individual who volunteers.

The one drawback for me is my tendency to get carried away by the possibilities. Then someone reminds me that the last thing we want is to have a lot of people signed up to help and nothing for them to do. It's part of my job to keep things in balance.

For Discussion

- How could our parish benefit from having a volunteer coordinator position?
- Where can we find more information about developing such a position for our parish?

CHAPTER TEN

Kingdom Now!

E aster came early that year and the weeks following were filled with the usual flurry that was part of preparing for all the sacramental celebrations of the season. Word had finally come from diocesan offices that Crosstown and Saints Alive parishes would not merge, but the bishop was mandating extensive collaboration instead. The two parishes would have a joint council as well as combined committees, activities, and programs. Father Ralph would be pastor for both. Parish leaders were surprised to discover how much the work of the volunteer ministry planning group had paved the way for the process.

With help from the new conciliation team and Father Ralph, people on the joint liturgy committee had worked through their differences with the new music director. People from each parish prepared liturgies together for the Easter season, planning in ways that made the most of both worship sites.

Though the purchase of a new organ had to be postponed, the rest of Saints Alive's remodeling project had been completed on schedule. Just yesterday, more than one hundred second graders from the two parishes had received their first Communion. This morning, as Nate entered the church, he couldn't believe how different everything seemed from the Sunday he'd first been there at Mass almost six years before. It wasn't just the rearrangement of pews or the addition of the new baptismal pool. There was a buzz in the air, a sizzle of conversation that reminded him of the sound he heard on windy days from the electrical wires that connected with the transformer behind his home. Clearly there were people gathered and, this time, he knew many of them personally.

Bill had greeted him at the entrance with a hearty handshake and, though Mass was beginning, Bill was still at the door, shaking hands with everyone who entered. He was taking courses to earn a certificate from the seminary now, preparing for a new career as a parish business manager. He still ran the ushers' program, though. In fact, he'd expanded it and doubled the number of volunteers scheduled for each Mass. Last fall the group had sponsored a day of reflection that focused on hospitality for all the liturgical ministries, office staff, and parish council members. Now ushers were scheduled to serve at whichever parish needed them most. Instead of trading boring reports at their meetings, they used some of the time to learn Spanish and become familiar with simple phrases of the Hmong people.

Cheryl and Doug rushed in breathless during the opening song, both infants and their toddler in tow. Harold moved over to make room for them in their pew while Adele scooped one of the babies into her arms.

After the psalm response, Marge Landowski read from the First Letter of John 3:1–2: *See what love the Father has bestowed on us in letting us be called the children of God! Yet that is what we are. The reason the world does not recognize us is that it never recognized the Son. Dearly beloved, we are God's children now; what we shall later be has not yet come to light....*

Nate smiled. As she did everything, Marge read with conviction. After attending half a dozen meetings with the volunteer ministry planning group, she had headed back to school, earned a certificate in human resource management and completed a certification process for volunteer administrators.

"I want your job, Morgan," she had informed him at the outset. "With what I'm learning at these meetings, I think I could do it pretty well."

Nate agreed. With help from Father Ralph, the volunteer ministry planning group was able to demonstrate how hiring Marge to coordinate parish-centered volunteers would benefit the collaborating parishes. She would officially start her new position in June.

Rosa and Mike, empty nesters now that their son Ramon had his own apartment, seemed younger and more energetic than ever as they carried up the gifts. Rosa was taking a year or two off from parish-centered volunteer work. The couple would soon be leaving for a long-saved-for trip to Vienna.

As they stood for the Our Father, Nate noticed that Glenna's family filled most of one pew. Her oldest daughter was home from college and it looked as if she had brought a young male visitor home with her. Nate assumed the older couple on Glenna's right was her mother and father. She had told Nate how difficult it had been for them being so far away when she needed support. Much to everyone's surprise, though, Glenna had found her own support. When the worst of the adjustment process was behind her, she single-handedly convinced the diocesan staff to pilot a divorce recovery program in the neighborhood, opening it up to people of all faiths in the area. She also made sure there was plenty of information available in the parish office about programs designed to strengthen existing marriages. When it was time for the sign of peace, Glenna was the first to cross the aisle and extend her hand to people on the other side.

When it was time for Communion, Nate's wife joined Janet and the other extraordinary ministers of holy Communion around the altar while Nate moved to stand at the side aisle so he would be available to chat with parishioners as soon as Mass ended. One by one, people filed forward, among them a boy, barely seven, in the white shirt and navy blue sport jacket he'd worn yesterday for the very first time. He walked stiffly, his hands folded solemnly in the formal position for prayer.

At the front of the line, he opened them to form a sort of cup and Janet placed the morsel of bread inside.

"The body of Christ," Janet said, smiling.

Joshua Alexander studied the bread for a moment, flashed a wide grin, then stuffed the bread into his mouth and headed jauntily back down the center aisle. Six steps later, he stopped short and whirled around, slapping his forehead then shooting his right arm high in the air.

"Amen! Amen!" he shouted. "I didn't say it, but I'll say it now! Amen! Amen!"

"Hush," whispered a stranger.

Crestfallen, Joshua Alexander clapped his hands over his mouth, slid into his pew, and disappeared among the assembly.

When Deacon Nate Morgan brought his understanding of the process model to the management of parish-centered volunteers, he also knew they would need a different way to evaluate progress. The cut-and-dried "if we can count it, it counts" evaluation techniques that served traditional management so well would fall short when taking discipleship into account.

Using traditional tallies, people who manage parish-centered volunteers could claim success whenever the number of recruits increased, when volunteers returned every year, when every task had enough warm bodies involved to complete it.

The word "evaluate" is rooted in words that mean "taking out from value." "More volunteers" is a value that can be important to parish life, but head count is far from the whole story. To sincerely evaluate their work, parish-based groups need to put what the group and community value into words in ways that can help them determine whether the work they do most effectively supports living out those values. Groups need to be very clear about what matters, then measure how effectively they are moving toward it.

Some of "what matters" will change little over time. Celebrating, proclaiming the Good News, serving, healing, and leading others to Christ, in other words, fulfilling the mission of the parish, will always be at the top of the list of "what matters" for every parish-based group. Some of "what matters," however, will change from year to year, from committee to committee, and from project to project. Each group is likely to have several "what matters" to prioritize. To be most effective, groups will decide early on, before they find themselves up to their earlobes in details and deadlines, the "what matters" in their projects, programs, and activities so they know for what they will hold themselves accountable. Consider this example.

Mary's Story

Mary, chairperson of the liturgy committee at a large suburban parish, was thrilled when she heard that the parish's liturgist had agreed to co-host a diocesan-wide liturgy conference. The diocesan staff would secure informative and inspiring speakers for the event. The parish's liturgy committee would provide everything else: planning, publicity, hospitality, administrative assistance, lunch, set-up, clean-up, whatever was needed.

The liturgist saw the event as an opportunity to bring up-to-date ideas to professional colleagues. Mary saw the event as a wonderful adult education opportunity for volunteers in nearly every area of parish life. In addition to liturgy and music professionals, she hoped to fill the space with liturgy committee volunteers from around the diocese, volunteers with a variety of interests from several nearby parishes, and others who might simply be curious. The liturgist and liturgy committee agreed and decided to hold the conference in the church where there would be plenty of seating.

As planning progressed, however, it became clear that little effort would be made to involve non-professionals. Every bit of the committee's energy was consumed with handling site details. Each time planners met, Mary raised the issue of encouraging more volunteers to register; each time she grew more frustrated with the response. The conference would be announced in area parish bulletins. The parish staff could copy and distribute the registration form they received. In the liturgist's opinion, that was publicity enough. If volunteers were interested, he reasoned, they would show up.

On the day of the event, the church was only half full. In front of Mary and the diocesan staff, the parish liturgist commented that it was too bad volunteer planners hadn't been able to convince more volunteers to come. He also passed responsibility for some minor glitches in the conference's logistics back to volunteer committee members. Mary left the event, hurt and exhausted.

Two weeks later, the planning committee tallied the conference evaluation sheets that reported good speakers, good food, a comfortable temperature in the meeting room, nice opportunities to network with colleagues. Once more, Mary raised the issue of volunteer participation. This time she was caught off guard by the liturgist's response.

"We didn't quite break even on the event, it's true," he said. "But neither the parish nor the diocese expected this to be a fund-raiser. Rated on a scale of one to five, the conference averaged a 4.2. I would say that's quite good."

Was the conference a success? It all depends on your point of view. The parish liturgist would say yes. His colleagues came and enjoyed what they experienced. From his perspective, the conference, which he valued as a way to inform and inspire liturgy professionals, did just that.

Mary, on the other hand, would say no. She thought more people should have been at the conference and not just to fill up the space or ensure that the event would break even. She thought that hosting the event at a parish instead of in the diocesan center would serve to inform and inspire a broader base of participants, including many volunteers. Since planners had never discussed volunteer attendance in terms of the income it would produce, Mary had no idea that that was how volunteer participation was being valued. Mary also knew that volunteer planners had experienced a lot of frustration over the event. From Mary's value perspective, the conference was a dismal failure. More important, she now mistrusted the liturgist's whole approach to working with volunteers. Mary decided she could no longer bring her best to the liturgy committee and planned to resign at the end of her term of service.

Whose values were the right values to measure? It doesn't matter. In parish life, many legitimate values surface. Those that support the parish in effectively fulfilling its mission deserve equal consideration, but groups need to clarify and agree on which values will be priorities in their projects, programs, and activities. Early on, groups need to plan to evaluate effectiveness accordingly, to *measure what matters*. The process of measuring what matters includes five steps.

- *Name what you value.* As soon as you have completed preliminary planning, discuss the values you hope to live out by completing this project. Are you hoping for high attendance? A chance to strengthen relationships in the faith community? Participation from people in other parishes? More money? A solution to a problem? A chance to learn something? Set judgments aside. Just name the values you want your project to support. In *Mary's Story*, at least two values were named beforehand: (1) inspiring and informing liturgy professionals; (2) inspiring and informing parish-centered volunteers from a variety of interest areas. A third value, "breaking even," wasn't raised until after the event.
- *Prioritize.* Put the values you named in their order of importance. Maybe you hope to raise a little money by charging a fee for a particular program, but your primary reason for sponsoring the program is to provide an adult

education opportunity. Be sure everyone involved understands "what matters." Be sure to also consider your parish's long- and short-range plans. Your priorities need to support the fulfillment of those plans, not use parish resources to move in a different direction. If people in your group don't agree on "what matters," now is the time to hash it out. In the example above, that conversation didn't happen. The liturgist prioritized one value; Mary struggled to make her value a priority as well.

- *Write them down.* Putting something in writing makes it real. Writing down "what matters" also makes it easier for the group to remember what they are holding themselves accountable for. Though Mary raised the issue of promoting the program among volunteers at every meeting, the idea just got tossed around verbally, a situation that happens often in parish meetings. Had the committee put "what matters" in writing, they would have had the opportunity to clarify and agree on what values were most important in this project, what they would hold themselves accountable for. That would have given everyone a choice—to work wholeheartedly toward the agreed-upon values or to pull back.

  Having a written statement of "what matters" in front of them at meetings would also help group members measure progress as they go and make adjustments accordingly.

- *Tell your public the truth.* If "what matters" is making money, communicate honestly about that. Just because the project is happening in a parish, you don't have to muddy the message by discussing or publicizing it in terms of how well it will build community. Telling the truth about what you really value *in this project* will help you attract volunteers with the skills you need and let the volunteers who would rather support different values invest their energies elsewhere. In the example above, Mary might have given less energy to the conference if she had understood that the primary goal was to inform and inspire liturgy professionals. As it turned out, though the liturgist undoubtedly meant well, Mary felt manipulated into working hard for something that wouldn't result in what she valued.

- *Measure what matters.* Once you have prioritized and written down "what matters," you know what to evaluate, what your group is holding itself accountable for. Though you can be flexible, don't let your group get sidetracked by outside lures. What "lures" come up often in parish life?

  Downplay the lure of $$$. Someone spots an opportunity to make a little more money from home visits to promote evangelization or a way to reduce people-related expenses on an event valued for its community-building impact. Before you know it, the bulk of your time, energy, and resources are going into the money-making or money-saving angles. "Evangelizing" and "strengthening community" fade into the background.

Downplay the lure of numbers. Filling the room is wonderful but, if "what matters" is helping people become more comfortable with sharing their faith stories or walk through a life-changing experience, high attendance isn't an appropriate measure of success. To really know if your project is effective, you will have do some qualitative evaluating.

Hint: In a situation like this, one way to determine whether "what matters" happened is to use a "before and after" questionnaire. Ask participants to answer no more than three questions related to your purpose at the beginning of a session. Then ask them to answer the same three question at its conclusion. Comparing the responses is likely to give you worthwhile information about the effectiveness of your approach.

Downplay the lure of "should." Someone in your group says its not appropriate for a faith-centered organization to do pure fund-raising or for a meeting to not be opened and closed with formal prayer. Before you know it, your promotional materials are studded with churchy sounding buzz and prayer has lost its meaning as a way to ask for help from the Holy Spirit in decision-making. Sooner or later, someone is bound to notice the mixed messages. The price is a real loss of trust.

"Should" is a dangerous word when it comes to managing volunteers. When you hear it, sound the alarms; raise red flags. Consider whether what you think you "should" be doing supports or hinders the process of discipleship for individuals and for the organization as a whole.

Downplay the lure of NOW! Because leaders want to be respectful of school and holiday calendars, many parishes tend to operate on a sort of semester system. Whatever can't be accomplished between September and June falls through the cracks. It is difficult to bring about significant change in such a limited time frame.

Hint: The liturgical calendar, with its simple rhythms that respect the natural processes of seeding, waiting, growing, dying, and being born anew, offers an alternative way to set up a timetable that will serve most parish projects well.

The volunteer ministry planning team in this resource allowed themselves plenty of time to wait, learn, and prepare, time to celebrate small successes and the promise of good things to come. They handled ordinary tasks as they arose, learned to let go of their own agendas, to die and rise, then begin all over again from a new experience of faith.

That kind of process didn't happen in Mary's story. Though driven by a clear, inflexible deadline, the committee might have benefited from incorporating some fallow time, some letting go time, some celebration time into their planning agenda.

Downplay the lure of "perfect." Similar to the lure of *NOW!* the lure of "perfect" tends to distract parish groups from completing projects they can't do really well. Rather than invest their energies in something that won't be perfect (or at least better than last year or better than the way the parish next-door does it), they spend their time lamenting shortfalls of time, space, money, people, and commitment. Though rarely named, "doing this perfectly" often ranks high on the values list in parish projects. As a result, creative ideas are frequently rejected before they have a chance to put success at risk.

Hint: When "what matters" requires doing something better, measure with continuums. Using word pictures or symbols, put "where we are" at the far left; and "where we want to be" at the far right of a straight line you've drawn on paper. Mark the steps needed to get from "here" to "there" on the continuum. Decide which step you can reasonably reach within a given time frame. When you reach it, celebrate! Then decide on a reasonable time frame for reaching the next step.

Downplay the lure of the expected. Even in an organization where discipleship is a core practice, the way things have always been done and the results those ways produce are powerful distractions. Choosing to try a new approach at the risk of not meeting historical expectations may leave your group looking or feeling as if it has failed. In Mary's story, wanting to meet the expectations of the diocesan staff may have been an unspoken factor that influenced "what matters." Another influence may have been a low level of expectation for volunteers, believing that few were able to understand the material being presented at the conference.

If the volunteer ministry planning group in this resource had let themselves be distracted by the lure of the expected, they would have responded to pressure to "beef up" recruitment in the short-term and might never have given themselves permission to step up to discipleship.

Hint: Working with continuums can dilute the lure of the expected. Most important in a Spirit-driven organization is to be sure that "honoring the unexpected" ranks somewhere high on list of prioritized values. If you draw a continuum, add a word picture or symbol that will remind you to look for "Surprise!" all along the line.

Volunteer Ministry Planner 10: Measure What Matters

In our parish, which of the above "lures" is most likely to distract volunteers from "what matters?"

❏   the lure of $$$
❏   the lure of numbers
❏   the lure of "should"
❏   the lure of NOW!
❏   the lure of "perfect"
❏   the lure of "expected"
❏   other lures:

As someone who manages parish-centered volunteers, how can you help volunteers deal with this distraction and measure what matters?

_____

_____

Pick a specific project on which you are working with a group. Work through the process of deciding what you will hold yourselves accountable for, how you will measure your effectiveness.

- *Name what you value.* List all of your goals and values for the project, everything you hope it will accomplish for the parish and for yourselves as you work together.

- *Prioritize and write them down.* Clarify and agree on "what matters" most to the effectiveness *of this project.* Plan to put most of your energy and resources into achieving those priorities and hold yourselves accountable for evaluating those priorities first.

    1. _____
       _____

    2. _____
       _____

    3. _____
       _____

- *Determine which "lures" are most likely to distract you from those priorities.*
  _____
  _____

- *Decide how will you deal with the distractions.*
  _____
  _____

- *Choose tools with which to measure your effectiveness.*
  ___ evaluation form
  ___ survey
  ___ face-to-face feedback
  ___ continuum
  ___ "before and after" questionnaire
  ___ recognition of surprises

Micro-Perspective

Talk with ____, the person you named on page 10 who is currently volunteering. Discuss "what matters" to that person relative to being managed as a volunteer. You can use the components in this resource as a starting point for your discussion.

Talk with _____, the person you named on page 10 who isn't currently volunteering. Discuss "what matters" to him or her in parish life. If you were to change one thing in how you manage for parish-centered volunteer ministry based on ____'s suggestions, what would it be?

∼

Watching from the side of the worship space, Nate Morgan realized that nothing in his first years as a deacon had happened as expected. He was used to that now. He planned thoroughly, just as he had in his corporate job, but in this place he had also learned to leave Spirit space in his plans, room for mystery to unfold. He could help volunteers manage their work, he could help them discover those unexpected places where gladness and hunger collide, but that was all. The rest was up to the Holy Spirit. Plans would change. The work would change. People would change. He would change. In this place, that was, after all, what mattered.

But, until this moment, Nate hadn't given much thought to the question that started it all, the question with which the volunteer ministry planning group had wrestled when they first tried to state their vision: *When volunteer ministry is thriving here, how will the parish be different when people are gathered to celebrate Eucharist?*

Nate let the question float out of his consciousness as he watched the extraordinary ministers of holy Communion return to their places among the assembly. Instead of returning to her own pew, Janet sat next to the stranger. Nate chuckled softly. Janet undoubtedly intended to introduce herself that morning. Before long, the gifted networker would have made a new friend who in time would be invited more fully into the journey of discipleship.

Bill squeezed into the pew already crowded with Glenna's family and gave Joshua Alexander a bear hug. "Way to go, Josh," he said out loud. "Great 'Amen!'"

Father Ralph blessed the gathering and sent the assembly on its way. The people were singing now, a song calling on the Holy Spirit that was one of Nate's favorites. By the time they reached the second verse, groups of God's people were streaming from their pews, spilling out of the doors into the rest of the world. But many, yes many, Nate noted with surprise, were still singing!

Nate watched as Father Ralph took his place among them, then he let himself be swept up into the kingdom and joined in the refrain.

Bibliography

Bass, Dorothy C., ed. *Practicing Our Faith: A Guide for Conversation, Learning, and Growing*. San Francisco, CA: Jossey-Bass Publishers, 1977.

DePree, Max. *Leadership Is an Art*. New York: Dell Publishing, 1989.

———. *Leadership Jazz: The Art of Conducting Business Through Leadership, Followership, Teamwork, Touch, Voice*. New York: Dell Publishing, 1992.

Donnelly, Doris, ed. *Retrieving Charisms for the Twenty-First Century*. Collegeville, MN: Liturgical Press, 1999.

Drucker, Peter F. *Management Challenges for the 21st Century*. New York: HarperBusiness, 1999.

Morgan, Gareth. *Imaginization: New Mindsets for Seeing, Organizing, & Managing*. San Francisco, CA: Berrett-Koehler Publishers, Inc., 1997.

Mueller, J.J. *Practical Discipleship: A United States Christology*. Michael Glazier, 1992.

Schein, Edgar H. *Career Anchors: Discovering Your Real Values* (workbook edition). San Francisco, CA: Pfeiffer and Company, 1990.

Senge, Peter. *The Fifth Discipline: The Art and Practice of the Learning Organization*. New York: Doubleday, 1992.

——— and Richard Ross, Charlotte Roberts, Bryan Smith, Art Kleine. *The Fifth Discipline Fieldbook: Strategies and Tools for Building a Learning Organization*. New York: Doubleday, 1994.

Thomas, R. Roosevelt. *Redefining Diversity*. New York: Amacom, 1996.

Westley, Dick. *Good Things Happen: Experiencing Community in Small Groups*. Mystic, CT: Twenty-Third Publications, 1992.

Zemke, Ron with Claire Raines and Bob Filipczak. *Generations at Work: Managing the Clash of Veterans, Boomers, Xers, and Nexters in Your Workplace*. New York: Amacom, 2000.

Other Related Liguori Publication Titles

Stewardship
A Parish Handbook
C. Justin Clements
ISBN 0-7648-0662-9

How to Share Your Faith With Others
A Good News Guidebook
Father Joseph T. Sullivan
ISBN 0-7648-0665-3

Rituals and Icebreakers
Practical Tools for Forming Community
Kathleen O'Connell Chesto
ISBN 0-7648-0407-3

Keepers of the Light
A Parents' Guide to Passing on Your Faith
Phyllis Calvey
ISBN 0-7648-0644-0